ATTILA, KING OF THE HUNS AND HIS PREDECESSORS: A HISTORICAL TREATISE
BY
William Herbert

1. Introduction.

If the extraordinary individual, who styled himself not unjustly the scourge of God and terror of the world, had never existed, the history of the Huns would have been very little more interesting to us at the present epoch, than that of the Gepidae, or Alans, or any of the chief nations that were assembled under his banner; but the immensity of the exploits, and the still greater pretensions of that memorable warrior, render it a matter of interest to know the origins of his power, and the very beginnings from which his countrymen had arisen, to threaten the subjugation of the civilized world, and the extirpation of the Christian religion. There has probably existed, before or since the time of Attila, but one other potentate, who, in his brief career, passed like a meteor over Europe, building up an empire, that was maintained by his personal qualities, and crumbled to atoms the moment he was withdrawn from it, leaving, however, consequences of which it is difficult to calculate the extent or termination.

One of the greatest losses that the history of Europe has sustained, is that of the eight books of the life of Attila, written in Greek by Priscus, who was his cotemporary and personally acquainted with him, and who, by the fragments that have been preserved to us, appears to have been most particular, candid, and entertaining, in his details. The loss is the more to be regretted, as it is certain that they did exist entire in the library of the Vatican after the restoration of literature, though it appears to have been ascertained by anxious research, that they are no longer to be found there; and there seems reason to suspect, that they may have been purposely destroyed through the jealousy of the Church of Rome, lest their publication should bring to light any facts or circumstances, that might militate against its policy or doctrines; when we consider the conspicuous part which was acted by the bishop of Rome, at the close of the Italian campaign of Attila, a period not long antecedent to the claim advanced by his successors to religious and political supremacy.

As we are thus deprived of the great fountain of information, our materials relating to the events of some of the most important portions of his life, and especially the particulars of its termination, are lamentably deficient. Under these circumstances it will be necessary to compare the brief and conflicting notices which have descended to us, with the copious and varied details of the most rude and ancient romances of Europe, which, however involved in confusion, and discredited by fiction and anachronism, can scarcely be supposed to have been built upon no foundation. The little we know concerning the origin and early habits of the Huns, is chiefly derived from Chinese writers who were consulted by Des Guignes, which may be compared with the statements of ancient chroniclers, and, as far as relates to the general manners of the Huns and other tribes that emerged from Asia, is most strikingly confirmed by Latin authority.

2. Origin of the Huns; fabulous account.

Two different accounts have been given by the old chroniclers of the origin of the Huns. The one, that they were descended from Magog the son of Japhet, brought forth by his wife Enech in Havilah, fifty-eight years after the deluge; the other, that the two branches of the Huns and Magyars were derived from Hunor and Magor, elder sons of Nimrod, who settled in the land of Havilah (meaning thereby Persia), and, having followed a deer to the banks of the Maeotis, obtained permission from Nimrod to settle there. By the agreement of all writers, the Huns were Scythians, and if the Scythian tribes were descended and named from Cush, son of Ham, the Huns could not have been of the blood of Japhet. A singular fabulous origin has been attributed to them.

Filimer king of the Goths, and son of Gundaric the great, having issued from Scandinavia and occupied the Scythian territory, found certain witches amongst his people, who were called in their language Aliorumnae or Alirunes, and he drove them far from his army into the desert, where they led a wandering life, and, uniting themselves with the unclean spirits of the wilderness, produced a most ferocious offspring, which lurked at first amongst the marshes, a swarthy and slender race, of small stature, and scarcely endowed with the articulate voice of a human being. It rarely, if ever, happens that a very old tradition is entirely without meaning or foundation, and it may perhaps be drawn from this absurd fable, that the Huns were of mixed descent between the Goths and Tartars.

3. Language of the Huns uncertain.

Great and formidable to all Europe as the Huns were in the reign of Attila, it is a matter of doubt what language they spoke. Eccard is quoted by Pray as arguing that they were Slavs, and used the Slavonic tongue, because Priscus only mentions two barbarian languages, as having been spoken in the camp of Attila, which were the Gothic and Hunnish; and he observes, that if the Slavonic and Hunnish had not been identical he would have mentioned the former also.

Pray, anxious, as are all the Hungarian writers, to identify the ancient Huns with the Avares of a later period, with the Magyars, and their own countrymen, argues against this, asserting that the Slavs did not enter Dalmatia and Illyria, till the time when the Avars were in Hungary, about a century after the days of Attila, and that the Tartars, to whom he refers the Hunnish origin, are not Slavonians.

There were, however, certainly Sarmatian nations under Attila, of which the Quadi may be particularly mentioned, and the words of Ovid distinguish the Sarmatian from the Gothic, as much as those of Priscus do the Hunnish language. But in truth Priscus does not say that only two languages were spoken, though he names the Gothic and Hunnish as prevalent, and perhaps as being only dialects of one tongue, for he nowhere asserts them to be radically distinct; and a brief examination of ancient evidence will perhaps lead us rather to consider it as a Teutonic dialect, than allied to the modern Hungarian. Priscus invariably uses the word Scythian, to include the Gothic nations with the Huns, and, if they were radically different in language as well as appearance, it is very difficult to understand how they should have been so classed under one denomination. He speaks also of their singing Scythian songs, which would convey no distinct meaning if the Scythians had two languages as widely different as the Gothic and Hungarian. In three other passages he mentions the language of the Huns. He says that on the embassy, with which he was himself associated, Maximin took with him Rusticius, "who was skilled in the tongue of the barbarians, and accompanied us into Scythia". Whenever he speaks of the Huns specially, he calls them Huns. He says of Zercon the buffoon, that, "mixing the tongue of the Huns and that of the Goths with that of the Italians, he kept the whole court, except Attila, in incessant laughter"; concerning which it may be observed, that, if the Hunnish and Gothic were not merely dialects of one language, the jests of Zercon could have been intelligible to very few of Attila's soldiers, and could scarcely have kept the whole court in a roar of laughter. In the other passage he says, "The Scythians, being a mixed people, adhere to their own barbarous tongue, either that of the Huns, or that of the Goths, or even those who have intercourse with the Romans, that of the Italians, but they do not readily speak Greek, except the captives from Thrace and the maritime part of Illyria". This is the sum of the information transmitted to us concerning their language, which seems to point rather to kindred tongues, like those of the Danes and Swedes which are easily understood by either nation, than to two languages radically different.

In the account given by Priscus of his progress through the north of Hungary with the embassy, he states that they were furnished instead of wine, with what was called by the natives meed, writing the word in Greek medos; and as those natives were the very Huns of Attila, near his principal residence, it affords a strong reason for attributing to them a Teutonic dialect, though the word kamos which he mentions for a sort of beer is not so easily traced. The name of Alirunes or Alrunae given to the mothers of the Huns, and stated by Jordanes in the first century after the death of Attila to have been the name used by the peo-ple amongst whom they originated, is decidedly a Teutonic word, which may be found in the Scandinavian Edda, written aulrunar. Jordanes tells us that the Huns called their fortified seat in Pannonia Hunniwar, which is indubitably Teutonic, the last syllable being the word which, according to the dialect, is called ware, ward, or guard, from which last form of the word our court is derived. The king, who led the Huns into Europe, is named by Jornandes, Balamber or Balamer, which is actually the same name as that of Walamir king of the Goths under Attila, whom Malchus calls Balamir. We know from the history of Menander that the river Volga was called Attila, or as the Greeks write it Atteelas, in German Ethel, in which form the name is connected with the Teutonic edel, noble; and the name of king Attila in the oldest German is Etzel, in which form it is possibly connected with the Teutonic steel, alluding to the sword-god, which with a similar deduction from the Greek chalybos, has been called chalybdicos, chalib, and excalibar. The documents, which could clear up the point, are probably lost beyond all chance of recovery, but it seems questionable whether the nationality of modern Hungarians has not induced them to claim a connection of blood with the Huns of Attila, to which they are perhaps not entitled.

Desericius in his voluminous work has exerted himself to demonstrate that the Huns had no affinity with the Alans, Goths, Gepids, Vandals, and Lombards, and they were certainly a race differing in stature and color from the Alans, which proves them to have been long distinct, though they may have branched out at a period later than the dispersion of mankind in the time of Peleg; but they dwelt near to each other, and their habits and worship were precisely the same. The question above proposed is whether their language was a dialect of the general Teutonic tongue spoken by those nations, (perhaps even an admixture of that with some other language) or radically and entirely distinct like the modern Hungarian. The oldest account we have of the Scythians is given in detail by Herodotus, about 450 years before the birth of Christ; 380 years after Christ Ammianus Marcellinus described the Alans who were of the Gothic family, with manners exactly similar to those of the Huns, and the same sword-worship which had been described as used amongst the Scythians by the father of profane history; and in the following century we find Attila the Hun, obtaining great reverence by means of a like sanctified sword, and making the very Scythian sacrifices described by Herodotus, and the Huns and Goths still called promiscuously Scythians by the Greek writers. The Teutonic nations and the Huns had therefore during at least 900 years before the death of Attila been known under one common denomination, and entertained the same habits and a similar religion; and it will not easily be proved that their languages had no affinity, by those who wish to establish the identity of the Huns and Hungarians.

4. Habits and manners of the Huns in the 4th Century.

The Hunnish nation, says Ammianus Marcellinus in the fourth century, little known by ancient records, and dwelling nigh the frozen ocean beyond the Meotian marshes, exceeds every known degree of savageness. From their very infancy their cheeks are gashed so deeply with steel, that the growth of the beard is impeded by scars; they grow up, like eunuchs, without beards or manly beauty. The whole race have compact and firm limbs, and thick necks, a prodigiously square stature, like two-legged beasts or stumps coarsely shaped into human figures.

They are so hardy, that they require neither fire, nor seasoned victuals, but live on the roots of wild plants, and the half-raw flesh of any sort of cattle, which they quickly warm by placing it under them on the backs of their horses.

They never frequent any sort of buildings, which they look upon as set apart for the sepulchers of the dead, and, except in case of urgent necessity, they will not go under the shelter of a roof, and they think themselves insecure there, not having even a thatched cottage amongst them; but, wandering in the woods from their very cradle, they are accustomed to endure frost, hunger, and thirst.

They are clothed with coverings made of linen and the skins of wood mice stitched together, nor have they any change of garment, or ever put off that which they wear till it is reduced to rags and drops off.

They cover their heads with curved fur caps; their hairy legs are defended by goat skins, and their shoes are so ill fitted as to prevent their stepping freely, on which account they are not well qualified for infantry; but, almost growing to the backs of their horses which are hardy and ill-shaped, and often sitting upon them after the fashion of a woman, they perform any thing they have to do on horseback. There they sit night and day, buy and sell, eat and drink, and leaning on the neck of the animal take their slumber, and even their deepest repose.

They hold their councils on horseback. Without submitting to any strict royal authority, they follow the tumultuous guidance of their principal individuals, and act usually by a sudden impulse. When attacked they will sometimes stand to fight, but enter into battle drawn up in the figure of wedges, with a variety of frightful vociferations. Extremely light and sudden in their movements, they disperse purposely to take breath, and careering without any formed line they make vast slaughter of their enemies; but, owing to the rapidity of their maneuvers, they seldom stop to attack a rampart, or hostile camp.

At a distance they fight with missile weapons, most skillfully pointed with sharp bones. Near at hand they engage with the sword, without any regard for their own persons, and while the enemy is employed in parrying the attack, they entangle his limbs with a noose in such a manner as to deprive him of the power of riding or resisting. None of them plough, or touch any agricultural instrument.

They all ramble about like fugitives without any fixed place of abode with the wagons in which they live, in which their wives weave their dark clothing, cohabit with them, bring forth their children, and in which they rear the boys to the age of puberty. Faithless in truces, inconstant, animated by every new suggestion of hope, they give way to every furious incitement.

They are as ignorant, as irrational animals, of the distinction between honesty and dishonesty, versatile and obscure in speech, influenced by no religious or superstitious fear, insatiably covetous of gold, so fluctuating arid irritably that they often fall off from their companions without any sufficient cause, and reconcile themselves again, without any steps having been taken to pacify them. Such were the Huns when they burst into Europe about the year 374 after Christ, and such they had been from the earliest period of history.

5. Chinese accounts of the Huns.

After the confusion of tongues in Sennaar (2247 BC) the Huns are said to have migrated into the mountains of Armenia and Georgia. Thence, emerging into the plain between the Tanais and Volga, they divided, part to the east, and part to the west. What became of those who travelled west does not appear, if the Huns are to be considered as distinct both from the Teutonic and Slavonian races. We read in some writers of dark and white Huns; the former being undoubtedly the Huns proper, and the latter some of the yellow haired tribes like the

Alans, who dwelt in their vicinity with habits very similar. The Huns who travelled eastward led a pastoral life, enclosed amongst the mountains, and had no intercourse with other nations, but perpetual warfare with the Chinese, from whom the only information concerning them is derived.

The Chinese make mention of the Huns 2207 BC dwelling to the NE, of China, feeding on the flesh of their flocks and dressed in skins. In their dealings with other people their affirmation held the place of an oath. They punished murder and theft, that is amongst themselves, with certain death. They accustomed their children to hunt and use arms. In their earliest years they shot birds and mice with arrows; growing bigger they pursued hares and foxes. No one amongst them could be deemed a man, till he had slain an enemy, or was bold and skilful enough to do so. It was their custom to attack their enemies unexpectedly, and to fly as rapidly when it was expedient. The great speed of their horses facilitated this mode of warfare, and the Chinese, who were accustomed to standing fight, could not pursue and vanquish them: and the Huns, if defeated, retired unto desert places, where the enemy would find it very grievous to follow them.

They were quite illiterate; their weapons were bows and arrows, and swords. They had more or fewer wives according to their means, and it was not unusual for a son to marry his stepmother, or a brother the widow of his brother. The Hun who could rescue the body of a slain comrade from the enemy became heir to all his property. They were anxious to make captives, whom they employed in tending their flocks. Thieves amongst other nations, they were faithful to each other.

They lived in tents placed upon wagons. The ancient Huns adorned their coffins with precious things, gold, silver, and jewels, according to the rank of the deceased, but they erected no tombs. Many servants and concubines followed the body at the funeral, and served it as if living; troops of righting men accompanied it, and at the full moon they began combats which lasted till the change. Then they cut off the heads of many prisoners, and each of the fighting men was rewarded with a measure of wine made from sour milk.

6. Hunnish kingdom from 210 BC, till the 4th Century.

Teuman, who reigned after the death of Chi-Hoam-tio, 210 years before Christ, over the Huns between the Irtish on the west, and the Amur, which rises in the mountains to the east of lake Baikal, and flows into the sea opposite Kamtchatka, pressed the Chinese on his southern confines, which appears to be the earliest specific action of the Huns upon record. He was killed by his son Meté, who took the title of Tanjoo or Tanju, meaning son of heaven. Whatever be the etymology of the name Tanju, coming to us through the Chinese historians, we cannot rely upon it as being a Hunnish title expressed in the Hunnish language. Some of the names they give of the ancient Hunnish potentates are so decidedly and radically different from the names borne by Hunnish princes in Europe, that they must be looked upon as

Chinese or Tartar versions of the names, rather than as the very appellations by which those persons were distinguished amongst their countrymen, unless their language underwent a complete change in the course of a few centuries after this period.

It is certainly possible that the Huns, if they had originally some affinity to the Tartars, as their personal appearance seems to indicate, having after centuries of connection with other Tartar races, been expelled by them from their seats, and having in their turn subdued their Gothic neighbors, may have gradually renounced much of the language of their invaders and adopted in great part the speech of the more humanized people who by conquest had become associated with them. The abode of the Tanjoos was in the mountains of Tartary.

On the first moon of the year the grandees of the empire or principal officers, each of whom commanded ten thousand men, assembled to hold a general council at the court of the Tanjoo, which ended with a solemn sacrifice.

At the fifth moon they met in another place, and sacrificed to Heaven, and Earth, and the Manes of their ancestors. In the autumn they assembled at a third place to number the people and cattle. The Tanjoo every day proceeded into the open plain to worship the sun, and every evening in like manner adored the moon. The title used by the Tanjoo, when he wrote to the emperor of China, was, the great Tanjoo of the Huns, engendered by Heaven and Earth, established by the sun and moon. The tent of the Tanjoo was on the left hand, as the most honorable place amongst the Huns, and it faced to the west. We know from Priscus that, when he visited the court of Attila, the seats on his right hand were considered the most honorable, and those on his left of secondary consideration; by which it appears that even in their highest ceremonials the Huns of his time had departed from their ancient custom, and adopted that which prevailed amongst the Goths. Mete was a successful prince, and extended the limits of his kingdom.

In the year 162 BC the Huns vanquished the people called Yue-chi, settled along the Gihon, who were afterwards called Jeta or Yetan, and were identical with the Getae. These adored Buddha, and carried the worship of Woden, who is the same Deity, into Europe; and, being of the Gothic race, they perhaps in some measure engrafted their habits and language on those of their ferocious conquerors. The empire of the Tanjoos having gradually increased, and having been maintained by frequent contests with various success against the Chinese, began to decline about the time of the birth of Christ, and in AD 93 it was entirely overthrown, the Tanjoo being defeated in battle, taken, and beheaded.

The Sien-pi Tartars occupied their territory, and many of the Huns mingling with them took the name of Sien-pi. The rest migrated westward into the country of the Baschkirs. This empire of the Huns, who are not mentioned by the Chinese as being a Tartar race, is said to have subsisted, from 1230 years before, till 93 years after the birth of our Savior, but the succession of Tanjoos is only known since 210 BC.

In 109 the Huns occupied Bucharia, and the country between the Gihon or Oxus, and the Irtish. In 120 they defeated the Iguri to the south, and killed the Chinese general who led them. In 134 they were themselves defeated by the Iguri, and in 151 they were driven further west by the Sien-pis.

In 310 we are told that, Lieou-toung king of the Huns having fallen in love with the widow of his father, she answered his passion, but was so bitterly reproached by her own son, that she died of vexation. This circumstance, transmitted to us amongst the scanty records of Hunnish transactions, militates directly against the accusation made against them by some modern writers of utter indifference concerning all incestuous connections.

It seems that the queen, mother of the heir to the throne, being dead, the king had taken to his throne another wife who had thereupon the rights of queen, and was not inheritable like the numerous wives of secondary condition who replenished the harem. Her submitting to the passion of her stepson was therefore probably regarded not only as an improper connection, but as a degradation from the rank and station she occupied as widow of the king. It is not improbable that the first wife enjoyed the rights of queen, on whose death the lady next espoused might succeed to her privileges; but we have no certainty that the wife, who was to have especial rights, and whose issue were to inherit, may not have been selected by the choice of her husband from the multitude of his wives.

In 316 Lieou-yao king of the Huns took prisoner a general of the Tsin Tartars, and invited him to a feast. On receiving the royal invitation, the captive warrior answered that he was so grieved by the disasters of his country, that he would rather die than survive them. Thereupon he was immediately accommodated with a sword and destroyed himself. Having failed in his first gracious intentions towards his prisoner, the monarch next turned his attention to the widow of the Tartar, who had also fallen into his hands, and was very beautiful, and he proposed to marry her: but the lady rejected his kindness with the same Spartan repugnance as her husband, whom she declared herself unwilling to outlive. The Hunnish monarch was equally scrupulous of thwarting her inclinations, and he was reduced to the gratification of burying them both in the most pompous manner.

In 318 the Topa Tartars gained possession of the country east of the Irtish. At this period the Tanjoo had his principal abode in the land of the Baschkirs, but his territory extended east to the Hi, and stretched westward to the Caspian. The Sien-pis confined them on the east, and the Topas driving the Sien-pis on the Huns, forced the latter further westward. On the south and south-west they were stopped by the Persians. From about the birth of Christ to the time of Valentinian the first (AD 364) the Alans had inhabited the lands between the Volga and the Tanais.

7. Nations bordering on the Huns before they entered Europe.

Ammianus Marcellinus, who died soon after the Huns entered Europe, states that the Alans occupied in his time the immeasurable and uncultivated wastes of the Scythians beyond the Tanais, taking their name from that of a mountain. The Neuri inhabited the midland parts near some abrupt hills, which were exposed to the north wind and severe frost. Next to them dwelt, the Budini, and the Geloni, a warlike people who flayed their slain enemies and made coverings of the human skins for themselves and their horses.

The Agathyrsi bordered on them, who dyed both their bodies and their hair with blue spots; the lower classes with few and small marks, the nobles with thicker spots more deeply stained.

The Melanchaenae and Anthropophagi were said to wander on the skirts of these nations, devouring their captives, and a large tract reaching to the north-east towards the Chinese was understood to be left unoccupied by the withdrawal of various tribes from the vicinity of those ferocious marauders.

The Alans had spread themselves very widely towards the east, where they had many populous tribes, who reached even to the banks of the Ganges. Like the Huns they had neither plough, nor cottage; they lived on flesh and milk, in wagons with curved coverings of bark. When they arrived at a grassy district, they arranged their wagons in a circle, and as soon as the grass was consumed, they shifted their quarters. The plains which they frequented were very productive of grass, and interspersed with tracts that bore apples or other fruit, which they consumed when occasion required. Their tender years were passed in the wagons, but they were early habituated to ride, and esteemed it disgraceful to walk, and were all by instruction skilful and expert warriors.

They were universally tall and well made, with yellowish hair, and remarkable by their eyes, in which ferocity was tempered with a more pleasing expression; swift in their movements, lightly armed, and much like the Huns in everything, but more polished in their dress and mode of living, making inroads both to hunt and plunder, as far as the Cimmerian Bosporus, and into Armenia and Media. Perils and warfare were their delight; the slaughter of a man their highest boast; and they reviled with bitterness those who lived to old age or died by accidents, esteeming it blessed to fall in battle. They fastened the hairy scalps of their enemies to their horses for trappings and ornament. They erected no temples, but planted a naked sword with barbarous rites in the ground and worshipped it as the protector of the district round which they had arranged their wagons. They had a singular mode of divining by collecting together a number of straight twigs, and after a time separating them again with some sort of incantation. Slavery was unknown amongst them; and the whole nation was considered to be of noble blood. Their judges were chosen on account of the prowess they had shown in warfare.

8. Entrance of the Huns into Europe. Reign of Balamer. King Box.

Upon these nations the Huns were driven by the inroads of the Tartars, who continued to force them towards the west. In the interval between the years 318 and 374, advancing northward of the Caspian, they subdued the Alans, associating numbers of them with themselves, and forcing the rest to take refuge in Europe.

In 374 they crossed the Maeotian swamp, or at least the river Tanais, into Europe. They had long considered the marshes to be an impenetrable girdle, till one of their nation, named Baudetes, having adventured more than usual in pursuit of a stag, succeeded in penetrating through them, and on his return communicated the important intelligence to his countrymen. Bishop Jornandes says that the stag led on the hunters by occasionally stopping to entice them, till it had conducted them into European Scythia, which he verily believes the foul spirits from whom they were descended devised out of enmity to its inhabitants.

The Huns profited immediately by the discovery of this passage, which opened to them a new world, and, whether they really crossed the Maeotis stagnant and choked with reeds or the Tanais higher up, they soon pushed their victorious arms to the banks of the Danube. They immediately attacked and reduced the Alipzuri and several other tribes, not omitting to sacrifice a due proportion of the first captives they made, according to the Scythian custom, to the Sword-God whom they worshipped. The hideous appearance of their swarthy and cicatrized faces, their short, stout, and erect figures, the swiftness of their steeds, and the skill of their archers, spread dismay on all sides, and they came like a hurricane upon the several nations who were peaceably depasturing the European banks of the Tanais.

The Alcidzuri, Itamari, Tuncassi, and Boisci, were subdued on the first inroad; and the following season was fatal to the liberty of the European Alans, excepting such as preferred to migrate westward, and seek the protection or extort the toleration of the Romans. Every conflict was a source of increased power to the Huns, who compelled the nations they subdued to join with them in further invasions, and with the sword of the Alans, united to their own, they now attacked the Goths.

Ermanric was at that time sovereign of the Goths, a man of very advanced years, who was then lingering under the effects of a wound received from Sarus and Animius, brothers of Sanielh or Sanilda, whom he had caused to be torn asunder by wild horses, to avenge himself on her husband, a chieftain of the Roxolani, who had revolted from him. The conjuncture was favorable to the invaders, and their king Balamer attacked the broad and fertile lands of Ermanric, who after vainly attempting to defend them, put an end to his own life. The Ostrogoths were subdued, having been previously weakened by the secession of the Visigoths, who had applied to the Roman emperor Valens to give them a part of Thrace or Moesia, south of the Danube, preferring a nominal dependance on the Romans, to the heavier yoke of the

Hunnish invaders. The request was granted, and they were baptized into the creed of Valens, who was an Arian. Ermanric having perished, the Ostrogoths remained subject to the Huns, under the administration of Winithar or Withimir of the family of the Amali, who retained the insignia of royalty.

The Gepidae were reduced under subjection to the Huns at the same period, and so rapid was their progress, that, within two years after crossing the Moeotis, they wrested the Pannonias from the Romans, either by force of arms, or by negotiation. In 378 Fritigern, king of those Goths, who had inundated Thrace, being irritated by Lupicinus and Maximus, and pressed by famine, made war upon the Romans. He was assisted by the Huns and Alans whom he subsidized, and many actions took place with various success. Valens, alarmed at their progress, made a hasty peace with the Persians, and returned suddenly from Antioch to Constantinople. Gratian advanced with a considerable force to form a junction with the army of Valens, but the latter, confident of victory, and fearful of losing, or of sharing with Gratian, the luster of that success which he anticipated, rashly attacked the Goths and their allies at the twelfth milestone from Adrianople near Perinthus.

The Armenian cavalry were routed by the first charge of the Goths, and left the infantry completely exposed to the enemy. The attack of the horse was supported by a shower of arrows, in the use of which the Huns were particularly skilful, and the Roman infantry was completely routed and cut to pieces by the swords and billhooks of the barbarians.

Valens took refuge in a house, where he was burnt alive by his pursuers, a practice not uncommon amongst the Scandinavian nations.

Gratian, receiving intelligence of this disaster, immediately recalled from Spain Theodosius, who in the following year repaired the falling fortunes of Rome, and, both by successful conflicts and by conciliatory offers and presents, put an end to the war. The pacification was however of short duration, and in 380 Gratian, being molested by the Huns, obtained the assistance of the Goths whom he took into his service.

It was probably at this time, that Balamer king of the Huns violated the treaties be had made with the Romans, and laid waste many towns and much of their territory with his armies, stating that his subjects were in want of the necessaries of life. The Romans sent an embassy to him, and promised to pay him nineteen pounds weight of gold annually, on condition of his abstaining from a renewal of such incursions. Whether the Ostrogoths had taken part with the Romans or not in 380, Winithar soon after attempted to throw off the Hunnish yoke, and his efforts were eminently successful. In the first encounter he captured a Hunnish king called Box, together with his sons, and seventy men of distinction, all of whom he crucified, to terrify the rest of their countrymen. Nothing else is known concerning this Hunnish prince, but it seems that from the time of the invasion of Europe in 374 till the murder of Bleda by his brother Attila, the Huns were never governed by a sole king.

For a short time Winithar the Goth reigned independent; Balamer, with the assistance of Sigismund the son of Hunnimund the Ostrogoth, who continued faithful to the Huns, attacked him, but was discomfited in two successive engagements. In the third battle on the banks of the river Erac, Balamer killed him, having wounded him surreptitiously in the head with an arrow, as they were approaching to each other. The defeat of his partisans was complete. Balamer married his grand-daughter Waladamarea, and possessed the whole empire, a Gothic prince however ruling over the Ostrogoths under the authority of the Huns.

Hunnimund the son of Ermanric succeeded to Winithar, and fought successfully against the Suevi. His son Thorismond reigned after him, and in the second year after his accession gained a great victory over the Gepidae, but was killed by the fall of his horse. The Goths greatly lamented him, and remained forty years after his death without a king, Berismund his son having followed the Visigoths into the west to avoid the Hunnish ascendancy. Balamer died in 386, soon after his marriage, probably leaving no children, and it is not known who immediately succeeded him.

9. Bela, Cheve, Cadica, kings of the Huns.

The first king mentioned by the Roman writers after this period is Huldin, but nothing is detailed concerning him before the year 400.

It seems probable that the three kings Bela, Cheve, and Cadica, named by the Hungarians as having reigned simultaneously, belong to the reign of Balamer, and perhaps Bela was the real name of the king who was styled by the Romans Balamerus. Under them was said to have been fought a great battle at a place called Potentiana, which from its circumstances seems referable to the period when the Huns first occupied Pannonia, seven or eight years before the death of Balamer.

Bela, Cheve, and Cadica, pitched their camp upon the Teiss. Maternus, being at that time praefect of Pannonia, administered the affairs of Dalmatia, Mysia, Achaea, Thrace, and Macedonia. He solicited the aid of Detricus (Dietric or Theodoric), who then ruled over a part of Germany, and having collected a great miscellaneous force to resist the common enemy, they encamped at Zaazhalon in Pannonia, not far from the southern bank of the Danube, and remained posted near Potentiana and Thethis.

The Huns crossed the Danube below the site of Buda, surprised the allied army in the night, and routed them with great slaughter, and encamped in the vale of Tharnok. There the Huns were attacked in their turn, when the allies had rallied their scattered forces, and after a severe contest the Huns were compelled in the evening to recross the Danube and return to their former position, but the victorious army was too much weakened to pursue them, and, fearful of a fresh attack, retired to Tulna, a town of Austria in the neighborhood of Vienna.

It seems extremely improbable that a narrative so circumstantial and apparently impartial, though discredited by some modern writers, should be entirely fabulous, and the persons mentioned in it fictitious. It is evident, that it must be referred to the period when the Goths and Romans were acting together, that is the year 380, when, according to the Latin writers, the Goths asked the assistance of Gratian against the Huns, and when, according to Priscus, Balamer violated the treaties and laid waste much of the Roman territory; Balamer (perhaps identical with Bela) being the chief sovereign, Box, Cheve, and Cadica, inferior kings over portions of the Huns.

10. Mundiuc. Huldin. Radagais.

To Balamer probably succeeded immediately Mundiuc, the father of Attila, but nothing is known of the particular actions of his life, and he is never named as concerned either with or against the Romans, in any military operations. In 388 the Huns were employed by Gratian against the Juthungi in Bavaria, and destined to act against Maximus in Gaul. In 394 they sent auxiliaries to Theodosius mixed with Alans and Goths under Gaines, Sanies, and Bacurius. In 397 it seems that Theotimus, bishop of Tomi or Tomiswar in Bulgaria, converted some Huns to Christianity, and it is not improbable that these converts were the persons whom Rhuas and Attila redemanded and crucified. From about the year 400 till 411 Huldin commanded the Huns in immediate contact with the empire, but we have no reason for supposing him to have been sole monarch of the Hunnish nation.

In 400 he killed Gaines, and sent his head to Arcadius. In conjunction with Sarus who was king over a portion of the Goths, Huldin and his Huns afforded assistance to Rome in 406, when Radagais had invaded Italy. Radagais is said to have been the most savage of all the barbarian monarchs. So strangely were the various nations blended, who were set in motion by the irruption of the Huns, and the pressure of the Asiatic Alans and other tribes upon the pastoral nations of Europe, that it is not known of what people this mighty commander was originally the ruler. Probably he was king of the Obotritae, or some other nation in the neighborhood of Mecklenberg, where he was worshipped as a God after his death.

He has been styled by most writers king of the Goths, because a great part of his force was Gothic, but there is no reason to suppose he was a Visigoth, and he certainly was not an Ostrogoth. Orosius calls him a pagan and Scythian, which conveys no distinct information, and it is even not unlikely that he may have been a Slavonian. Whatever was his own nation, he had been a most successful adventurer, swelling his army with the fighting men of the tribes which he successively overthrew, and drawing others to his camp by the renown of his name, till he had collected an immense confederated army of Vandals, Sueves, Burgundians, Alans, and Goths. With this force he entered Italy, and laying waste the whole country north of the Po, he prepared to besiege Florence at the head of 200,000 soldiers; threatening that he would raze the fortifications of Rome, and burn her palaces; that he would sacrifice the most distinguished patricians to his Gods, and compel the rest to adopt the mastruca, or garment of skin dressed with the hair on, that was worn by some of the barbarous nations.

The approach of this formidable enemy filled the Roman capital with dismay: the pagans thought that under the protection and with the assistance of the Gods, whom he was said to conciliate by daily immolations of human victims, it was impossible for him to be overcome, because the Romans neither offered to the Gods any such sacrifices, nor permitted them to be offered by any one. There was a concourse of heathens in the town, all believing that they were visited with this scourge, because the sacred rites of the great Gods had been neglected. Loud complaints were made, and it was proposed to resume immediately the celebration of the ancient worship, and throughout the whole city the name of Christ was loaded with blasphemies; but the degenerate Romans were more disposed to curse and offer up sacrifice, than to fight in defence of the empire. A very small force was collected under Stilicho, and the defence of Italy was entrusted to Huldin with a Hunnish, Sarus with a Gothic, and Goar with an Alan, force of hired auxiliaries.

The prudent measures of Stilicho ensured their success. The invading army was camped on the arid ridge above Faesulae, ill furnished with water and provisions. Stilicho conducted his approaches with such skill, that he blocked up all the avenues, and rendered it impossible for the enemy to draw out his army in line against him. Without the uncertainty of a hazardous conflict, without any loss to be compensated by victory, the army defending Rome ate, drank, and were merry, while the invaders hungered, and thirsted, and pined away without hope of extricating themselves from their calamitous situation. Radagais despairing abandoned his army, fled, and was intercepted.

The conqueror has been accused of sullying the glory of this achievement, by the deliberate murder or execution of his prisoner. A third part of the army surrendered, and the captives were so numerous, that herds of them were sold for single pieces of gold, and such was their misery, that the greater part of them perished after having been purchased. The entire credit of the discomfiture of the invaders, is given by the writers of that age to the troops of Huldin and Sarus, and the Roman forces are not mentioned.

There were twelve thousand noble Goths whom the Latins called optimati in the army of Radagais, and with these, after the disaster of their leader, Stilicho entered into confederacy. It appears by the chronicle of Prosper, that the army of Radagais was separated in three divisions under distinct chiefs; one division only perished at Faesulae; the other two were untouched, and his remaining Goths were afterwards diverted by Stilicho into Gaul. It seems that there must have been treachery in the invading army, which was not unlikely to occur, seeing that it consisted principally of Goths, and that he was besieged by Goths under Sarus.

Supposing the two other divisions of the army of Radagais to have been faithful to him, it could scarcely be doubted that, when he quitted the troops who were surrounded at Faesulae, he was attempting to rejoin them, for the purpose of leading them on to raise the blockade, and was intercepted in that undertaking: but a due consideration of the subject will lead us to suspect that the account given by Aventinus is correct, that Huldin and Sarus had entered Italy in concert with Radagais, but were seduced from his authority by Stilicho. Their force must have been part of the two divisions which remained uncaptured, and the Goths of Sarus a portion of the very troops which Stilicho afterwards persuaded to remove their quarters into Gaul; for it is impossible otherwise to explain how a sufficient power of Huns and Goths could be at hand to oppose an army of 200,000 men, which had already overrun and laid waste all the north of Italy, and had placed itself between Stilicho and the dominions of the Huns. The probability is therefore strong, that Stilicho discomfited Radagais by means of his own auxiliaries, having by negotiation drawn off from him two-thirds of his army, and surrounded the remainder, which might have consisted of sixty or seventy thousand men nominally, but probably was already reduced by the rude invasion of a hostile country.

11. Charato.

From this period during some years the Huns do not appear to have manifested any decided hostility to the Romans. In 409 a small force of Hunnish auxiliaries assisted them to defeat Ataulfus, and in 410 Honorius appears to have hired a body of Huns to oppose the progress of Alaric, which is not surprising, as the Huns were certainly not united under any sole monarch, and both they and the Goths seem at that time to have been ready to assist the highest bidder. The peaceable demeanor of the Huns towards the empire is probably the reason that so little has reached us concerning their kings at this period.

No mention of Huldin occurs after the campaign against Radagais, and, although we are told that the Hunnish satellites or auxiliaries of Stilicho were destroyed when he himself was killed, we hear of no Hunnish king, till the brief mention which is made by Photius, in detailing the contents of the work of Olympiodorus, of Charato, chief of the Hunnish petty kings. The circumstances mentioned by him are certainly referable to the period between the usurpation of Jovinus in 411 and his death in 413.

Olympiodorus was sent on an embassy from Constantinople to Donatus and the Hunnish princes, whose marvelous skill in archery struck him with astonishment. Who Donatus was is not known, but he must have been either a Hunnish king, or a chieftain of some nation closely connected with them. Donatus was ensnared by an oath, probably of safe conduct, and unlawfully and treacherously put to death by the Romans. Charato the chief of the Hunnish kings was greatly exasperated, but the Romans contrived to appease his resentment by presents. Nothing further is known of Charato; he may have been the chief ruler of the Huns, or which is more probable, only the first of the petty kings under Mundiuc.

12. Aetius

From the year 413 no true historical competitor appears to contest the occupation of the Hunnish throne with Mundiuc, though a false king has been conjured up by Pray in his Hungarian annals, in the person of Rugas or Rhoilus. At this period the celebrated Roman Aetius was a hostage in the Hunnish court, having been previously three years a hostage to Alaric the Goth. It is most probable that he was given as surety to the Huns for the safe return of the auxiliary force which they sent in 410 against Alaric. He was the son of Gaudentius, by birth a Scythian or Goth, who had risen from the condition of a menial to the highest rank in the cavalry.

His mother was a noble and wealthy Italian, and at the time of his birth his father was a man of praetorian dignity. Aetius, having passed his youth as a hostage at the courts of Alaric and the Hunnish king, married the daughter of Carpileo, was made a count, and had the superintendence of the domestics and palace of Joannes. He was a man of middle size, of manly habits, well made, neither slight nor heavy, active in mind and limbs, a good horseman, a good archer and poleman, of consummate military skill, and equally adroit in the conduct of civil affairs; neither avaricious, nor covetous, endowed with great mental accomplishments, and never swerving from his purpose at the instigation of bad advisers; very patient of injuries, desirous at all times of laborious occupation, regardless of danger, bearing without inconvenience hunger, thirst, and watchfulness; to whom it is known to have been foretold in his early youth that he was destined to rise to great authority.

Such is the character given of him by a contemporary writer; to all which might have been added, that he was a consummate villain, a treacherous subject, a fake Christian, and a double dealer in every action of his life. In 423 his patron Joannes, known by the name of John the tyrant, (which title only implies that he possessed himself of unlawful authority) seized the opportunity of the death of Honorius to assume the sovereign power, and sent ambassadors to Theodosius, who threw them into prison. In order to strengthen himself against the attack which he had reason to expect, he dispatched Aetius, who was then superintendant of his palace, with a great weight of gold to the Huns, with many of whom he had become united by close ties of personal friendship, while he was a hostage at their court.

In 425 the Huns entered Italy under the guidance of Aetius. Their number has been estimated at 60,000. It is not known by whom they were commanded, though it has been asserted that Attila was then twenty-five years old and headed the expedition. At this critical moment Joannes was killed, and the subtle Aetius immediately made his peace with Valentinian, who was glad to receive the traitor into favor, on condition of his removing the formidable army of invaders from Italy. Having advanced in compliance with the request of Aetius, and already received the gold of Joannes, they were easily prevailed upon to withdraw by him who had conducted them, and they appear to have returned home without committing any outrages, which marks the great influence that Aetius had acquired over their leaders.

13. Rhuas.

It seems however most probable that they were commanded by Rhuas, who in the succeeding year threatened that he would destroy Constantinople, and probably made an incursion into the territory of the Eastern emperor, though the marvelous account which is given of the expedition by contemporary writers is a gross and palpable falsehood, which must be detailed only to be confuted.

Theodoret, who lived at the time when this event is said to have taken place, after speaking of the destruction of pagan temples and the general superintendence of Providence, says, "for indeed when Rhoilus the leader of the Nomad Scythians both crossed the Danube with an army of the greatest magnitude, and laid waste and plundered Thrace, and threatened that he would besiege the imperial city, and take it by main force, and utterly destroy it, God having struck him with lightning and bolts of fire from above, both destroyed him by fire, and extinguished the whole of his army".

Socrates, also cotemporaneous, writes to the following effect: "After the slaughter of John the tyrant, the barbarians, whom he had called to his assistance against the Romans, were prepared to overrun the Roman possessions. The emperor Theodosius, having heard this, according to his custom, left the care of these things to the Almighty; and, applying himself to prayer, not long after obtained the things which he desired; for what straightway befell the barbarians, it is good to hear. Their leader, whose name was Rugas, dies, having been struck by lightning, and a pestilence supervening consumed the greater part of the men who were with him; and this struck the barbarians with the greatest terror, not so much because they had dared to take up arms against the noble nation of the Romans, as because they found it assisted by the power of God".

Well indeed might the Huns have trembled, and all Europe have quaked even to the present day at the recollection of such a manifest and terrible interposition of the Almighty, if the Hunnish king with an immense army had been so annihilated, and, as Socrates proceeds to say, in pursuance of an express prophecy: but it is easy to demonstrate the falsehood of the narrative.

Theodoret immediately subjoins to the passage cited from him, that the Lord did something of the same kind in the Persian war, when the Persians, having broken the existing treaty and attacked the Roman provinces, were overpowered by rain and hail; that in a former war, Gororanus having attacked a certain town, the archbishop alone broke his lofty towers and engines to pieces and saved the city; that on another occasion a city being beleaguered by a barbarian force, the bishop of the place put with his own hands an enormous stone on a balista or engine called the apostle Thomas, and firing it off in the name of the Lord knocked off the head of the king of the barbarians, and thereby raised the siege. The fellowship of such tales takes away all faith from that which concerns the Huns. But according to Socrates, the event was prophesied by Ezekiel, and the prophecy applied previously by the bishop of

Constantinople; and here we arrive at the clue to explain how such a marvelous relation came to be credited.

"Archbishop Proclus (continues Socrates) preached on the prophecy of Ezekiel, and the prophecy was in these words—And thou, son of man, prophesy against Gog the ruler, Rosh Misoch, and Thobel; for I will judge him with death and blood, and overflowing rain and hailstones; for I will rain fire and brimstone upon him and all those with him, and on the many nations with him; and I will be magnified and glorified, and I will be known in the presence of many nations and they shall know that I am the Lord". This prophecy is put together from the second verse of the 38th ch. of Ezekiel. "Son of man, set thy face against Gog, the land of Magog, the chief prince of Meshech and Tubal, and prophesy against him", and the 22d and 23d verses, "I will plead against him…" The word Rhos upon which the application of this prophecy to the Hunnish Rhuas rested, occurs in the Septuagint, though it is not in the Vulgate, the word having been rendered by St. Jerome head, and applied to the following word, signifying the head or chief prince of Meshech. The archbishop was wonderfully praised for this adaptation of the prophecy, and, according to Socrates, it was the universal topic of conversation in Constantinople; and doubtless this adaptation gave birth to the marvelous history.

Rhuas had threatened to destroy Constantinople; while the people were expecting his attack, the archbishop assures them that God had expressly denounced by his prophet that he would destroy Rhuas and his people with fire and brimstone from heaven. Rhuas never came near Constantinople; the archbishop's prediction was confirmed in the important part that concerned the safety of its inhabitants, and the story became current that it had been entirely fulfilled, and that Rhuas and his army had perished accordingly. The story is confined to the Greek divines; not one of the Latin chronicles of that age mentions any expedition of the Huns under Rhuas against the Eastern empire. Bishops Idatius, Prosper, and Jornandes are silent; Cassiodorus and Marcellinus are silent; but if such a manifestation of the Almighty had occurred, or anything that could give color to such a belief had really taken place, Europe would have rung with the rumor of it to its very furthest extremities.

Procopius relates the death of John the tyrant, but nothing concerning Rhuas. To complete the refutation of the tale we learn from Priscus, who was sent on an embassy to the Huns from Constantinople, only twenty-two years after the date of the supposed catastrophe, that Rhuas was alive after the consulship of Dionysius which took place in 429, that is three years after the time when the divine vengeance is said to have overtaken him; and the chronicle of Prosper Tyro says that Rhuas died in 434. The Hungarian annalist, Pray, carrying absurdity to the highest pitch, and aware that Rhuas was alive in 429, asserts that there must have been two kings, one Rugas killed by fire from heaven, and another by name Rhuas his successor; and he accuses all foregoing writers of having confounded them, though there is not the slightest reason for imagining that there were two such kings, except the inconvenient circumstance of his being found alive long after the time when he should have been exterminated, to fulfill the prediction of the Byzantine prelate.

14. Rhuas and Octar. Obarses.

It is known from Jornandes (Jordanes) that Rhuas and Octar were brothers of Mundiuc and kings of the Huns before the reign of Attila, but that they had not the sovereign authority over all the Huns. The date of their accession is no more known than that of Mundiuc.

Pray, who is always expert in distorting the truth to support his own theory, assumes inaccurately from Jornandes that, on the death of Mundiuc, Attila his son was a minor, and that Octar and Rhuas his uncles had been appointed by his father to be his guardians. There is no authority for the supposition, excepting that Calanus says Mundiuc commended his sons with their portion of the kingdom to his brother Subthar.

Octar, otherwise called Subthar, and Rhuas were probably kings in conjunction with their brother. We do not know that Attila was not also a king during their life-time, which the expression of Calanus seems to imply, and even during his father's reign, for his own son had regal authority during his life-time. Octar and Rhuas did not reign over all the Huns, yet after their death and the murder of his brother Bleda, Attila was sole monarch, which seems to imply that Attila and Bleda were the kings who had reigned over those not subject to their uncles. The very circumstance of the joint reign of Attila and Bleda, till the latter was removed by murder, shows that brothers had a concurrent right of sovereignty amongst the Huns, and would lead us to conclude that Octar and Rhuas were associated with Mundiuc, and Calanus expressly says that Subthar (otherwise called Octar) did reign in conjunction with Mundiuc. Pray argues that if they held the throne in their own right, and not as guardians, Obarses, who is mentioned by Priscus as another son of Mundiuc, should have been a king also, which he does not appear to have been; but this is quite erroneous, for Obarses is not said to have been by the same mother; and it is clear, that although the Hunnish kings were allowed to indulge in polygamy, there was one queen with superior rights, whose children alone were entitled to succeed. Attila had a legion of wives and a host of children, but Priscus only mentions by name three sons, who were children of Creca whom he calls especially his wife and not one of his wives, and they alone succeeded to his dignities, though the other sons wished the kingdom to foe equally divided amongst them.

15. Burgundians.

In the obscure period of Mundiuc's reign, the first collision of the Huns with the Burgundians must have taken place, which led to events celebrated in the romantic legends of almost the whole of Europe north of the Danube, of which it is however very difficult to unravel the real history. The Burgundiones (supposed to be the Frugundiones of Ptolemy) had their earliest recorded kingdom near the Vistula, on the borders of Germany and Sarmatia. At that time Born-holm or Burgundar-holm in the Baltic seems to have been their sacred place of deposit for the dead, an island perhaps consecrated like Mona or Iona.

From the Vistula they appear to have advanced to the Oder, and having approached the Rhine in 359, as early as 413 they established themselves, 80,000 in number, on the Gallic side of that river. Athanaric is the earliest of their chiefs who is recorded to have reigned near the Rhine, marrying Blysinda daughter of Marcomir, who was the sire of Pharamond. His eldest son Gondegesil succeeded him, and dying, left the crown to his brother Gundioc or Gondaker, who had three sons, Gondegesil, Gondemar, otherwise called Gunnar or Gunther, and Gondebod.

The royal family of the Burgundians were called Nibelungian or Nifflungian, and were supposed to have brought with them a great treasure of gold which was probably removed from Born-holm. During the reign of Mundiuc the Huns made successful incursions into the territory of the Burgundians, plundered their towns, and reduced them to a state of dependence: The Arian priests took advantage of their miserable and depressed state to inculcate their doctrines amongst them, representing idolatry to be the cause of their reverses; whereupon the Burgundians embraced a qualified sort of Christianity, and were baptized into the Arian faith. Octar, after the death of his brother, proceeded in the year 430 with a large army of Huns into Burgundy to chastise their apostate and rebellious vassals; but he was defeated with great slaughter, and perished in the expedition, though probably not in battle. Elated by this success, the Burgundian king seems to have thought himself strong enough to fight single-handed against all opponents, and, instead of courting the alliance of any one of the great powers, disposed himself to make head against them all.

16. Exploits of Aetius.

When the unexpected death of John the tyrant had rendered abortive the invasion of Italy by the Huns under the guidance of Aetius, that skilful negotiator made his terms with Valentinian and Placidia, and the chief command of the army in Gaul was the reward which he immediately received for the dismissal of the Huns. In the very next year he delivered Arles from the Visigoths, and in 428 he recovered from Clodion, king of the Francs, the parts of Gaul near the Rhine which had been occupied by him, and in the following year he overpowered the Juthungi in Bavaria.

Having brought to an end the Vindelician or Bavarian war, in the autumn or the following spring he defeated the Burgundians who were pressing sorely on the Belgians, and on that occasion the Huns, Herulians, Francs, Sauromatians, Salians, and Gelons fought against him. This conflict must have taken place immediately before the disaster of Octar's army, when the Huns and their auxiliaries were probably invading some part of the Belgic territory, and the check they received on that occasion may have encouraged the Burgundians to revolt and overpower them.

In the year 432 Bonifacius his rival, who had been urged to acts of treason, and betrayed by the perfidy of Aetius, returned from Africa to Rome, and obtained the dignity of Master of the forces. A personal conflict took place between them, in which Aetius was worsted, but his antagonist died a few days after from the effects of a wound which he had then received. Aetius retired to his villa, but an attempt having been there made upon his life by the partisans of Bonifacius, he fled into Dalmatia, and from thence he proceeded to the court of Rhuas king of the Huns in Pannonia. The great influence, which he had obtained amongst them, had suffered no diminution, and at the head of a Hunnish army he once more threatened the throne of Valentinian. The Romans called the Visigoths to their assistance, but no engagement took place on this occasion; Placidia and her son submitted to the demands of Aetius, and he returned again with accumulated honors to command the army in Gaul. His antagonists were now the Burgundians, who must have provoked the Romans by making inroads or attempting to establish themselves on the territory of the empire; and in 435 he completely routed them with exceeding great slaughter, and forced their king to throw himself upon his mercy.

17. Death of Rhuas. Attila (his accession).

In the meantime immediately after the restoration of Aetius to favor, his protector Rhuas had died, and Attila had succeeded to the throne in Pannonia. His brother Bleda reigned over a portion of the Huns, apparently nearer to the confines of Asia. It is not known with certainty which was the eldest, the fact not being stated by any author of decisive authority; but as Priscus, whenever he mentions them in conjunction, places the name of Attila first, and Jornandes states that he succeeded to the throne with his brother Bleda, the presumption is very strong that Attila was the eldest.

The Hungarian writers who have attributed to Attila the extraordinary age of 124, state also that he was born and died on the same days of the year as Julius Caesar, and that he was seventy-two years old when he was made king, considering that he acceded to the throne in 402, and that he was an efficient commander of the troops, when the Huns entered Europe in 374. This monstrous absurdity is only surpassed by the assertion, that, after his death, a son, said to have been borne to him by the Roman princess Honoria, fled to the father of Attila, who was still living in extreme old age and debility.

The words of Priscus, who was personally acquainted with Attila, afford a decisive refutation to those who attribute to him extraordinary longevity and a protracted reign. He states on the authority of Romulus the father-in-law of Orestes, the favorite of Attila, with whom he conversed in the presence of Constantius who had been secretary to Attila, and of Constantiolus a native of Paeonia which was subject to him, that no king, either of the Scythians or of any other country, had done such great things in so short a time. The date of Attila's accession to the supreme power, at least over that portion of the Huns, which was in contact with the Romans, is fixed with great precision by comparing the words of two contemporary writers.

Priscus says that Rhuas, being king over the Huns, had determined to wage war against the Amilsuri, Itamari, Tonosures, Boisci, and other nations bordering on the Danube, who had entered into confederation with the Romans. Thereupon he sent Eslas, who had been accustomed to negotiate between him and the Romans, to threaten that he would put an end to the subsisting peace, unless the Roman would deliver up to him all those who had fled from the Huns to their, protection. The Romans, desirous of sending an embassy to Rhuas, fixed upon Plinthas of Scythian, and Dionysius of Thracian, extraction, both generals and men of consular dignity. It was however not thought expedient to dispatch the ambassadors before the return of Eslas to the court of his sovereign, and Plinthas sent with him Sengilachus, one of his dependants to persuade Rhuas to treat with no other Roman than himself. "But (continues Priscus) Rhuas having come to his end, and the kingdom of the Huns passed unto Attila, it seemed fitting to the Roman Senate, that Plinthas should proceed upon the embassy to them". Dionysius was not consul till 429, and the chronicle of Prosper Tyro fixes the death of Rhuas in 434. In that year therefore it appears that Attila succeeded to the throne of his uncle in conjunction with his brother Bleda, who ruled over a considerable distinct force of Huns, but may perhaps have resided near Attila in Pannonia.

The manner of the death of Rhuas is not recorded, the relation of his destruction by fire from heaven before Constantinople being disproved; but the language of Jornandes throws a strong suspicion upon Attila of having removed him by murder, for after mentioning his succession to his uncles, and relating that he slew his brother, to obtain an augmentation of power, he adds that he had proceeded by the slaughter of all his relatives. We have no reason to believe that any other relative stood between him and the supreme authority, and it is not credible that Jornandes should represent a single act of fratricide as the murder of all his family. It is barely possible, that, although Rhuas did not die by lightning before Constantinople, as alleged by the Greek ecclesiastics, it may have been given out by his murderers in 434, that he was struck by lightning, and that he may even have been destroyed by some explosion of chemical fire, as was probably the case with the emperor Carus, who is universally said by old historical writers to have been struck by lightning while lying sick in his tent; though it cannot be reasonably doubted, on reading the letter of his secretary, that he was murdered by his chamberlains.

18. Attila (his age)

The age of Attila at the time of his accession cannot be ascertained. Rejecting as absurd the accounts of his great age, we cannot assent to such an abridgement of his life as Pray has made, in order to accommodate his notion of an undivided and hereditary monarchy. Assuming that he must have been a minor when his father died, and forgetting that, if his uncles had occupied the sovereign authority merely as guardians, they would have been bound to resign it when Attila arrived at manhood, and that he was not of a character to live until twenty-six years of age, if unjustly excluded, without making any attempt to possess himself of his hereditary rights, he assigns twenty years to him, as the maximum of his age in 428, when his father died, and twenty-six when he succeeded Rhuas in 434. But he has entirely overlooked a circumstance which shows the inconsistency of this calculation; which is, that, if Attila by the Hunnish laws could not have reigned under the age of twenty-one, his son could not have done so; yet in 448 Priscus, having been at the court of Attila, relates the elevation of the eldest son of Attila and Creca by his father's directions to the throne of the Acatzires and other nations near the Euxine. If barely twenty-one in 448 he must have been born in 427, and Attila must have been married to Creca at least as early as 426, two years before the death of Mundiuc, at which period according to Pray's calculation he could have been but eighteen years old; and it would not be easy to show that the Hunnish monarch was likely to establish his son by marriage to that woman who amongst his numerous wives was to give heirs to the throne, while it was still deemed necessary to hold him in tutelage.

That Attila must have been married to Creca before the year 427 is all that we can ascertain; if barely twenty-one at that time, he must have been born as early as 406, and would have been twenty-eight when he succeeded Rhuas, but it is most likely that he was older. Creca was perhaps his first wife, and her children on that account heirs to the throne, and it is most likely that he was raised to the rank of a petty king during the life of his father. The old Scandinavian legends, concerning which more will be said hereafter, speak much of his residence at the court of Gundioc or Giuka king of Burgundy, (calling Attila by the name of Sigurd) and of his intimacy with Gundaker or Gunnar the Burgundian prince. In all these accounts he is described as the greatest warrior of his age. It is very probable that Attila was employed in the first subjugation of the Burgundians, and, while they remained in vassalage under the Huns, the young prince of Burgundy must, in the natural course of things, have served under Attila in his campaigns against the petty chieftains of the neighboring countries.

19. Treaty of Margus. Mama and Atakam.

In consequence of the death of Rhuas, by a decree of the senate which was approved by the emperor Theodosius, Plinthas was despatched to the court of Attila without Dionysius, and at his special request it was decreed, that Epigenes, who had served the office of quaestor, a man much considered on account of his learning, should accompany him. They proceeded to Margus a town of Moesian Illyria near the Danube, opposite the fortress Constantia which was on the northern bank, whither the two Hunnish kings had resorted. Attila and Bleda advanced without the walls on horseback, not choosing to receive the Roman embassy on foot.

The Roman ambassadors, consulting their dignity, mounted their horses also, that they might be on equal terms with the Huns; but, notwithstanding their momentary exaltation, they proceeded immediately to sign a most disgraceful treaty, which was ratified by the oaths of either party, according to the customary ceremonials of their respective countries.

The Romans bound themselves to send back to the Huns all those who, at however distant a period, had fled from their dominion and taken refuge under Roman protection, and also all Roman prisoners who had escaped from captivity whithout paying ransom, and in default of the restoration of any such prisoner, eight pieces of gold were to be given for each head to their former captors. They further promised to give no assistance to any barbarian nation, that should wage war against the Huns. It was agreed that trade should be carried on between the two powers on equal terms, and that peace should continue between them so long as the Romans failed not to pay seven hundred pounds weight of gold annually to the Huns, the tribute exacted until that time having been no more than three hundred and fifty pounds.

Thereupon the fugitives were actually given up, amongst whom were two youths of the blood royal, Mama and Atakam, who were immediately crucified in Carsus a fortress of Thrace, as a punishment for their flight.

20. Princess Honoria. Sorosgi. Litorius

In this year the Roman princess Honoria, having disgraced herself by an illicit connection with her chamberlain Eugenius, and her pregnancy having been detected, was expelled from the palace at Ravenna, and sent by her mother Placidia to Theodosius at Constantinople, where she was placed under the superintendence of his sister Pulcheria, who lived under a religious vow of celibacy, to which she adhered even when, after the death of her brother, she espoused Marcian as a support to the throne, but excluded him from conjugal rights. The princess, not less ambitious than devoted to pleasure, secretly excited Attila against the Western empire by the tender of her hand. He does not appear to have accepted the proposal at the time, and the offer was perhaps repeated at a later period, when it suited his plans to demand her in marriage. Having concluded peace on such advantageous terms with the Romans, Attila with his brother Bleda marched against some tribes of Scythians, who had either not yet submitted to the authority or had presumed to shake off the yoke of the Huns, and they immediately attacked the Sorosgi in the east of Europe. This expedition was undoubtedly attended with the success that usually crowned the arms of Attila, but the particulars of it have perished with the lost work of Priscus. Having reduced his Scythian adversaries, he turned his thoughts to avenge the overthrow of his uncle by the Burgundians, and in 436 he vanquished them with great slaughter and the loss of their sovereign.

In the year 437 the Romans, undoubtedly through the influence of Aetius, obtained the assistance of a body of Hunnish auxiliaries, who were conducted by the Roman general Litorius against the Visigoths then laying siege to Narbonne. The two armies were drawn up in line against each other, and showed the most determined countenance, and it seemed as if the fortunes of Theodoric must depend upon the issue of that day, but the collision of these formidable armies was suspended by negotiation, the Goths and the Huns shook hands upon the field of battle, and Attila was appeased by the concessions of the Visigoths. What advantages he obtained by this bloodless victory and the dereliction of the Roman interests, we are not informed by Jornandes who relates the circumstance, but he styles Attila at this period the sole ruler of almost the whole Scythian nation throughout the world, and of marvelous celebrity amongst all nations, a statement which very ill accords with the suggestions of Pray, who makes him a novice just emerged from the tutelage of his uncles.

Two years after however Litorius appeared again in the field against Theodoric at the head of an army of Huns, who seem to have been subsidized by the Romans. The Huns fought with their usual valor, and the victory was for awhile doubtful, but the unparalleled rashness and imprudence of Litorius rendered the exertions of his troops unavailing. He was taken by the Goths, and led ignominiously through the streets of Narbonne; the Hunnish auxiliaries were completely routed, and we do not hear of their ever again having acted in concert with the Romans. From this time we have no account of any proceedings of the Huns in Gaul, till the year of the great battle of Châlons, and the attention of Attila appears to have been principally directed against the Eastern empire.

21. Capture of Margus, Viminacium, Ratiara

It is exceedingly difficult to adjust the dates and particulars of the several events that are mentioned by different writers. The capture of Margus and Viminacium, which seems to have been the first act of hostility against Theodosius, has been referred by Belius to the year 434, immediately after the reduction of the Sorosgi, but it is not credible that Margus should have been captured by the Huns, immediately after the peace concluded there. On the contrary, the account of Priscus makes it evident that those events directly preceded a more important attack on the dominions of Theodosius, and they are clearly referable to the year 439, following immediately the disaster of Litorius in Gaul. During the security of a great annual fair in the neighborhood of the Danube, the Hunnish army fell unexpectedly on the Roman, seized on the fortress which protected them, and slew a great number of their people. Remonstrances were made concerning this flagrant breach of faith, but the Huns replied, that they were by no means the aggressors, because the bishop of Margus had entered their territory, and pillaged the royal domain; and that, unless he was immediately delivered into their hands, together with all the fugitives whom the Romans were bound by treaty to give up, they would prosecute the war with greater severity. The Romans denied the truth of their complaint, but the Huns, confident in their assertion, declined entering into proofs of their accusation, and, having crossed the Danube, carried war and devastation into the forts and cities of their enemies, and, amongst others of less importance, they captured Viminacium, a Mysian city in Illyria. So fallen was the spirit and vigour of the Roman empire, that, notwithstanding the alleged innocence of the bishop of Margus, it began to be pretty loudly suggested that he ought rather to be delivered up to the vengeance of the barbarians, than the whole territory of the empire exposed to their atrocities. The bishop, aware of his perilous situation, secretly passed over to the enemy, and offered to deliver up the town, if the Scythian princes would enter into terms with him. They promised him every possible advantage, if he would make good his proposal, pledging their hands and confirming the agreement by oaths; whereupon the bishop returned into the Roman territory with a great force of Huns, and having placed them opposite the bank of the river in ambush, in the night time he arose at the appointed signal, and delivered up the town to its enemies. Margus having been thus taken and sacked by the Huns, they became daily more formidable, and waxed in strength and insolence.

In the following year (441) Attila collected an army consisting specially of his own Huns, and wrote to the emperor Theodosius concerning the fugitives in the Roman territory and the tribute which had been withheld from him on occasion of the war, demanding that they should be instantly delivered up, and ambassadors sent to arrange with him concerning the payments to be made in future; and he added that if they made any delay or warlike preparations, he should not be able to restrain the impetuosity of his people. Theodosius showed no disposition to submit; he peremptorily refused to yield up the refugees, and answered that he would abide the event of warfare, but that he would nevertheless send ambassadors to reconcile their differences, if possible. Thereupon Senator, a man of consular dignity, was sent by the emperor to treat with Attila; he did not however venture to traverse the territory of the Huns even under the protection of the character of an ambassador, but sailed across the Euxine to Odessus, the modern Odessa, situated near Oczakow on its northern extremity, where the general Theodulus, who had been despatched on a like mission, was at that time abiding, without having succeeded in obtaining an audience. In what quarter Attila was then stationed, is not recorded, but he had probably advanced with his army, before the negociator reached his destination; for on the receipt of the answer of Theodosius, being greatly incensed, he made an immediate and sanguinary irruption into the Roman dependencies, and, having taken several fortresses, he overwhelmed Ratiaria, a city of great magnitude and very populous, which stood near the site of Artzar, a little below Vidin on the Danube. He was accompanied by his brother on this inroad, and they laid waste a great part of Illyria, demolishing Naissus, (Nissa) Singidunum, (Belgrade) and other flourishing towns. Seven years after, the sophist Priscus on his embassy to the court of Attila, passed by the desolated site of Naissus, and saw the ruins of that exterminated town, and the country strewed with the bones of its inhabitants.

22. Comet and pestilence in 44. Defeat of Arnegisclus at the Chersonese. Peace concluded by Anatolius

The succeeding campaign was ushered in by the appearance of a comet of great magnitude, which added to the terror of the Hunnish arms, and a fatal pestilence raged throughout Europe. The brothers renewed the ravage of Illyria, and stretched their victorious course to the extreme shores of Thrace. In this expedition only we hear of Persians serving under Attila together with Saracens and Isaurians, but it is certain that no part of Persia was reduced under his dominion, though the Bactrian king of the Caucasean Paropamisus is said to have been amongst his military vassals.

Arnegisclus was entrusted by Theodosius with a great army to stop the progress of the invader, but he was completely routed on the shore of the Chersonese; the enemy approached within twenty miles of Constantinople, and almost all the cities of Thrace, except Adrianople and Heraclea, submitted to the conqueror. The army, which was quartered in Sicily for the protection of the eastern provinces, was hastily recalled for the defence of Constantinople, and Aspar and Anatolius, masters of the forces, were sent to negotiate with the invaders, whose progress they had small hope of arresting in the field of battle. A treaty or rather a truce for a year was concluded with the Huns by Anatolius, according to which the Romans consented to give up the fugitives, to pay 6000 pounds weight of gold for the arrears of tribute, and the future tribute was assessed at 2100 pounds of gold; twelve pieces of gold were to be the ransom of every Roman prisoner who had escaped from his chains, and on default of payment he was to be sent back to captivity. The Romans were also compelled to pledge themselves to admit no refugees from the dominions of the Huns within the limits of the empire.

The ambassadors of Theodosius, too haughty to acknowledge the grievous necessity to which they were reduced, of accepting whatever terms the conqueror might think fit to impose, pretended to make all these concessions willingly; but, through excessive dread of their adversaries, peace upon any conditions was their paramount object, and it was needful to submit to the imposition of such a heavy tribute, though the wealth not only of individuals, but of the public treasury, had been dissipated in unseasonable shows, in reprehensible canvassing for dignities, in luxurious and immoderate expenditure, which would not only have been misbecoming a prudent government in the most prosperous affluence, but was especially unfitting for those degenerate Romans, who, having neglected the discipline of war, had been tributary not only to the Huns, but to every barbarian that pressed upon the several frontiers of the empire.

The emperor levied with the greatest rigor the taxes and assessments which were necessary to furnish the stipulated tribute to the Huns, and those even whose lands, on account of the destructive inroads of the barbarians, had been for a while discharged from the payment of taxes, either by a judicial decision, or by imperial indulgence, were compelled to contribute. The senators paid into the treasury the gold which was required from them beyond their means, and their eminent situation was the cause of ruin to many of them; for those, who were appointed by the emperor to levy the rate, exacted it with insolence, so that many persons, who had been in affluent circumstances, were forced to sell their furniture and the trinkets and apparel of the women. So grievous was the calamity of this peace to the Romans, that many hanged themselves in despair, or perished by voluntary starvation. The treasury being immediately emptied, the gold and the fugitives were sent to the Huns, Scottas having arrived at Constantinople from the court of Attila to receive them. Many however of the fugitives, who would not surrender to be delivered up to their inexorable countrymen, from whose hands they would have suffered a cruel and lingering death, were slain by the Romans to propitiate the enemy; and amongst those were some of the blood royal of Scythia, who, refusing to serve under Attila, had fled to the Romans.

23. Resistance of the Azimunthians.

Attila was not however contented with these severe exactions, but proceeded to summon the Azimunthians to surrender the captives they had taken from the Huns and their allies, and the Roman refugees whom they harbored, as well as those whom they had retaken from them. Azimus was a fortress of great strength, not for from the Illyrian frontier, but appertaining to Thrace. The inhabitants of this formidable post had not only resisted the attacks of the Huns within their walls, so that no hopes were entertained of reducing them, but had successfully sallied out against the invaders, and discomfited in many rencounters the numerous forces and most expert commanders of the barbarians. Their scouts traversed the country in every direction, and brought them sure intelligence of every movement of the enemy; and, whenever the Azimunthians received information that they were returning from an inroad laden with the plunder of the Romans, they concerted measures for intercepting their passage, and falling unexpectedly upon them, though few in number, by the most resolute and enterprising valor, aided by a perfect knowledge of the intricacies of the country, they were usually successful, and not only slaughtered many of the Huns, but rescued the Roman prisoners and gave shelter to the deserters from the pagans.

Attila therefore declared that he would not withdraw his army, nor consider the conditions of the treaty fulfilled, until the Azimunthians should have dismissed all their captives, and delivered up to him the Romans who were in the fort, or paid the stipulated ransom.

Neither Anatolius by negotiation, nor Theodulus by the array of the army which was entrusted to him for the protection of Thrace, could divert Attila from this determination, for he was enhardened by success, and ready in a moment to recommence his operations, while they were dejected and discouraged by the recent disaster.

Letters were therefore sent to Azimus, requiring them to liberate their captives, and to send back the Romans who had been rescued, or twelve pieces of gold in lieu of each of them. The Azimunthians replied that they had suffered the Romans, who had fled to their protection, to depart at their pleasure, but that all the Scythian captives had been slain; excepting two whom they retained, because the Huns, after having for a while besieged their fortress, had placed themselves in ambush, and carried off some children who were tending the flocks at a short distance from the walls, and that, unless those were restored, they would not give up the captives they had made in war.

Enquiries were instituted concerning these children, but they were not forthcoming, and, the Hunnish kings having made oath that they had them not, the Azimunthians set free their captives, and swore likewise that the Romans had departed from amongst them; but they swore falsely, the Romans being still in the fortress, while they held themselves absolved from the guilt of perjury by the countervailing merit of having saved their countrymen. It appears from this account, which is detailed by Priscus, that the Azimunthians were a hardy race in possession of an impregnable mountain hold, where they rendered a very qualified allegiance to the emperor, and probably closed their gates against his tax-gatherers.

24. Sword of the War-God. Style and pretensions of Attila. Engaddi. Danes. Second Moses in Crete. St. Patric

About this period, probably in the campaign of 442, Attila asserted that he had possessed himself of the ancient iron sword, which from the earliest recorded time had been the God of the Scythians. A herdsman, tracking the blood of a heifer which had been wounded in the leg, was said to have discovered the mysterious blade standing erect in the sod, as if h had been flung forth from heaven, and carried it to Attila, who received it as a fresh revelation of the sword of Ares or Areimanius which had been worshipped by the ancient Scythian kings, but had long disappeared from earth. He accepted it as a sacred badge and evidence that the power of the spirit of war was committed to him, and a certain presage of the approaching universality of his dominion.

The prevailing expectation of the advent of the Messiah, mankind being greatly ignorant of the true character of Him who was to come, had encouraged Octavius Caesar to assume the title of Augustus, and pretend to divine honors; and it was perhaps not merely the flattery of his courtiers, but the real opinion of those who expected a divine revelation at that period, that represented him as a present God.

The era of Attila was marked by a very general expectation of the revelation of Antichrist. It has been already mentioned that it was prophesied to Aetius in his youth that he was to be some great one; by which expression is meant a divine incarnation.

Symmachus in his panegyric of Gratian amongst his orations discovered and edited by Maius, stated about sixty-five years before that he heard the prophets of the Gentiles were whispering, that the man was already born, to whom it was necessary that the whole world should submit; that he believed the presage, and acknowledged the oracles of the enemy.

There seems to have been a strong opinion entertained in Italy that the fortunes of Rome could only be upheld by making her the head of the barbarous nations and of all paganism, and in this spirit Symmachus had pleaded before Valentinian in 384 against Christianity, and, as his oration is styled, on behalf of his sacred country. The great object of this party in Rome was to give a Roman ruler to the Gentiles, instead of receiving an emperor from them. With this view the traitor Stilicho, a nominal Christian, educated his son in paganism and the most bitter animosity against the Christians.

When Radagais invaded Italy, the people looked to Stilicho for salvation, and it was carried by acclamation in Rome, that the neglected rites of their ancient Deities must be immediately renewed. After Honorius had cut short the traitor, dispersed his barbarian satellites, and driven into banishment his panegyrist the poet Claudian, who was a decided pagan, and probably died at the court of some heathen king, Aetius became the head of this party, with like views and deeper villainy. To him it had been prophesied that he was the great one whom the nations were expecting. His son Carpileo was sent to be educated amongst the heathens; he had, by long residence both at the Gothic court of Alaric and amongst the Huns of Attila, familiarized himself with all the leading characters of Europe.

The pious and eloquent Prudentius was too remote from these odious machinations to have suspected the sincerity of Stilicho, and saw in him only the savior of the empire and defender of Christianity; and it is probable that with like hypocrisy Aetius, whose wife was certainly a Christian, imposed on the credulity of Leo, who appears to have highly regarded him; which is the least creditable circumstance known concerning that pontiff. Exerting his great military talents no further than suited his hidden views, and balancing all the powers of Europe with the nicest artifice, that no one might obtain the universal dominion which he expected ultimately to snatch from them all, he proceeded steadily in his object, till Valentinian cut him short at the moment when the death of Attila had probably determined him to declare himself.

The minds of all men both in the Roman empire, and amongst the heathen nations of Europe, being thus strongly tinctured with the expectation of the revelation of a predestined and distinguished person, who was to establish a new and prevailing theocracy, the importance of assuming that character to himself could not escape the penetration of Attila; and it is not impossible, that, educated as he was in the cradle of superstition, he may have believed that the great destinies to which he pretended were really awaiting him. We learn from Jornandes, who quotes the authority of Priscus, that he acquired very great influence by the acquisition and production of the venerated sword. The title which he assumed is said to have been, Attila, grandson or rather descendant of the great Nembroth or Nimrod, nurtured in Engaddi, by the grace of God king of Huns, Goths, Danes, and Medes, the dread of the world. He is represented on an old medallion with teraphim or a head on his breast

We know from the Hamartagenia of Prudentius that Nimrod with a snaky-haired head was the object of adoration of the heretical followers of Marcion, and the same head was the palladium set up by Antiochus Epiphanes over the gates of Antioch, though it has been called the visage of Charon. The memory of Nimrod was certainly regarded with mystic veneration by many, and by asserting himself to be the heir of that mighty hunter before the Lord, he vindicated to himself at least the whole Babylonian kingdom.

The singular assertion in his style that he was nurtured in Engaddi, where he certainly never had been, will be more easily understood on reference to the twelfth chapter of Revelation concerning the woman clothed with the sun, who was to bring forth in the wilderness, "where she hath a place prepared of God", a man-child, who was to contend with the dragon having seven heads and ten horns, and rule all nations with a rod of iron.

This prophecy was at that time understood universally by the sincere Christians to refer to the birth of Constantine who was to overthrow the paganism of the city on the seven hills, and it is still so explained: but it is evident that the heathens must have looked upon it in a different light, and have regarded it as a foretelling of the birth of that great one, who should master the temporal power of Rome. The assertion therefore that he was nurtured in Engaddi, is a claim to be looked upon as that man-child who was to be brought forth in a place prepared of God in the wilderness. Engaddi means a place of palms and vines in the desert; it was hard by Zoar, the city of refuge, which was saved in the vale of Siddim or demons, when the rest were destroyed by fire and brimstone from the Lord in heaven, and might therefore be especially called a place prepared of God in the wilderness, like the garden of Amalthea, in which Bacchus was fabled to have been brought up. That such a title was either actually assumed by Attila, or given to him by those who favored his pretensions, may be established by the total ignorance of the historians who have recorded it of its meaning, and the extraordinary fact being stated by them without any comment Engaddi was also the seat of the Essenian cenobites, that remnant of the inhabitants of Sodom, who before the advent of our Savior had set the example of the most profligate abominations under the mask of holiness and austerity; and a fitter cradle could hardly have been devised for an Anti-christian adventurer.

He was certainly not king over the Medes, but the title was probably assumed when he had been on the point of undertaking an expedition to reduce them, which Priscus ascertained to have been his intention, and would probably have been carried into execution, if his life had been prolonged. Notwithstanding the vague accounts of early Danish history, which have been put together from Scandinavian legends, the name of Danes appears to have been scarcely known before this period.

Servius, whose commentary on Virgil had perhaps been then written a little more than twenty years, probably makes the first mention of the name, saying that the Dahae, a people of Scythia adjoining to Persia on the north, were called also Dani. Picrius writes concerning the same passage, that the Dahae and Dacians were the same people. Jornandes a century after the time of Attila, first names the Danes in Denmark, stating them to be a distinguished race of superior stature amongst the Codani, with whose name that of the south of the Baltic, called Sinus Codanus, is identical.

Procopius gives an account of the migration of the Herulians from the vicinity of the Danube through the tribes of the Danes into Thule, the modern Thylemark. Nicolas Olaus says that he found it stated in an old Hungarian chronicle that the Danes formerly inhabited the region of Hungarian Dacia, and betook themselves to the maritime parts of the north of Europe through fear of the Huns. If the Dacians who had migrated northwards bore at that time the name of Danes on the coast of the Baltic, they were not of sufficient importance in themselves to have merited such a particular mention in the title of the great monarch, unless because he actually occupied Dacia.

It is however exceedingly probable that the particular mention of Danes, had reference to the prevailing opinion that Antichrist was to be of the tribe of Dan, founded upon the prophecy of Jacob in the 49th chapter of Genesis, "Dan shall be a serpent by the way, an adder in the path, that bites the horse's heels, so that his rider shall fall backward. I have waited for thy salvation, O Lord", which last words seem to imply that the posterity of Dan would not await it, as Jacob had done, and from the circumstance of the tribe of Dan not being sealed in Revelation.

We are informed by several writers that in the reign of Attila, a certain mysterious person, who is called a second Moses in Crete, that is coming in the spirit of Moses, deceived the Jews in that island, pledging himself to lead them back through the sea with dry feet to the land of promise. Those who linked themselves together by the hair, and sprang off a cliff into the sea at his suggestion, all perished; a few were converted to Christianity and escaped. The Rabbis and rabbinists assure us that there cannot be a second Moses, coming in the power of Dan, unless his soul be an emanation of Cain the fratricide. Postel states that the Moses in Crete was such an one as Antichrist. Werner Rolewink in his fasciculus temporum makes the second Moses synchronize with Patric's voyage to Ireland.

Father Colgan, in his Trias thaumaturge, says that the magic wand, which was transmitted by Adam and Nimrod to Moses, passed into the hands of Jesus Christ, and from him was transmitted to Patric; who spent forty days and forty nights in a mountain, fasting and conversing with God, saw God in a burning bush, and died at the same age as Moses, (viz.

120) and his eye was not dim, nor his natural strength abated; and from these and other coincidences, he is called the second Moses.

St. Patric is also said to have summoned all the serpents and venomous creatures to the top of a mountain over the sea and bade them jump down, and they were all drowned. It cannot be over-looked on reading the several passages relating to the second Moses, that the story appears to have a more intimate connection with the affairs of Attila, than is stated on the face of any one of the extracts; for the writers proceed immediately from the narration of Attila's acts to this strange account, and again from it to Attila's invasion of Gaul. Whether such a man as Patric actually existed, and was sent on a secret mission by Attila to prepare the way for himself as Antichrist, as we read in the Scandinavian sagas that Attila sent Herburt on a mission to king Arthur in Great Britain, or whether Patric was merely a fictitious name used by those in Ireland, who looked to the coming of Attila as Antichrist, to represent his power and his kingdom, it may be difficult to determine; but the Cretan tale seems to be connected with the legend of St. Patric, and that legend to have reference to the expectation that Attila would establish an universal antichristian dominion. When we are told that a person deceived the Jews with the expectation of leading them back to the land of promise, coming as a second Moses, and such an one as Antichrist, that no second Moses could come in the power of Dan, except an emanation from the soul of Cain the fratricide; that Attila affected particularly the title of king of the Danes, and that he did murder his brother like Cain, and attempt to establish an antichristian universal empire, we have some reason to conclude that Attila did pretend to come in the power of Dan, and in the spirit of Moses as a lawgiver.

25. Murder of Bleda. Predicted duration of the Roman empire.

Having thus arrayed himself with superhuman pretensions, as predestined to overthrow that empire, which, in compliance with the predictions of the Sibyl, Romulus was said to have consecrated with the blood of Remus, Attila proceeded soon after to murder his brother Bleda. The exact mode of his death is not known; he is said to have been slain and cast into the Danube; according to one account a dispute arose concerning the name to be given to the new town of Sicambria, which either brother wished to call after his own, and the modern Buda is said to be a version of the name Bleda. The tradition of the twelve birds seen by Romulus and the six seen by Remus, bears a strong appearance of having been founded on some true prophecy concerning the duration of the ever memorable Roman empire, and it is very remarkable that Attila murdered his brother Bleda, and may be supposed to have consecrated by his blood the new city of Sicambria, which he intended to make the seat of a new empire to supersede that of Rome, exactly twelve centuries after the alleged revelation of the twelve birds to Romulus; 755 being the years of Rome before Christ, and 445 after Christ, the date of the murder of Bleda, making exactly twelve centuries from his death to that of Remus. If we add six single years for the six birds of Remus, it brings us to the year 452 on which Attila, master of nearly all Italy, was expected to enter Rome; if instead of six single years we add six lustra or periods of five years by which the Romans were wont to number the lapse of time, it brings us precisely to the year 476 in which the Roman empire was finally extinguished by Odoacer.

It is not easy to believe that such wonderful coincidences are accidental, especially when we recollect that this is not a subsequent interpretation of the augury, built upon the events that actually took place, but it had been thus explained in the oldest times; and, as the period drew near, the most learned men, both heathen and Christian, were looking for its accomplishment, and it is not unlikely that Attila used for his ensign a vulture bearing a golden crown with reference to the birds of Romulus. Varro, as cited by Censorinus, had written that he had heard Vettius a distinguished augur and a man of great genius and learning say, that if the facts related by historians concerning the foundation of the city by Romulus and the twelve vultures were true, the Roman state would endure twelve hundred years, since it had already survived the 120th year.

The pagan poet Claudian who was contemporary with and involved in the ruin of Stilicho, had stated that the people dreading the invasion of the Goths counted the years numbered by the twelve vultures, and from the expiration of the twelfth century anticipated the overthrow of Rome. Sidonius Apollinaris bishop of Clermont, who wrote a few years after the death of Attila alluded in two passages to the fate prognosticated to Rome by the twelve vultures. It is therefore quite certain that Attila must have been aware of this prediction, and of the interpretation which was given to it by Christians and pagans at this period, and had been handed down from remote antiquity; and it is as certain that such a circumstance must have had great weight with a man attempting to establish an empire which was to supersede that of Rome, and to be built in like manner upon the worship of the sword-god Mars; and it can scarcely be doubted that this prediction and a consideration of the received history of Romulus had its share in exciting him to murder his brother Bleda.

Aiming at the establishment of universal dominion by the influence of superstition and religious awe, as well as by the force of arms, he could no more have overlooked the fact, that the twelve centuries of Romulus were actually expiring in the year when he followed his fratricidal example, than it had escaped the flatterers of Augustus that in his time the seventy weeks of Daniel were expiring amidst the intense expectation of the nations.

26. Attila overruns all Thrace. Arnegisclus slain in battle. Trace concluded. Attila chastises the Acatzires. Curidach.

The same year that witnessed the elevation of Attila to the sole power amongst the Huns by the removal of his brother, brought a fresh attack upon the Eastern empire, though neither the causes which led to the renewal of hostilities, nor the events of the campaign have been handed down to posterity. After a pause of one year, probably obtained by fresh concessions from Theodosius, the war was renewed on a greater scale than ever in 447.

The forces of the Western empire afforded no assistance to their Eastern brethren, and not less than seventy cities were taken and ravaged by the Huns. It was a fierce contest, and greater than the former wars of the Huns; the castles and towns of a large tract of Europe were leveled to the ground. Arnegisclus made a memorable stand against Attila and fought valiantly, but fell in the battle, and the total discomfiture of his army left the whole of Thrace at the mercy of the conqueror. In this campaign the celebrated Arderic king of the Gepidae distinguished himself under Attila, who was supported by the Ostrogoths and a portion of the Alans, and various other nations serving under their respective kings.

The whole extent south of the Danube, from Illyria to the Black Sea, was ravaged by the Huns, whose army swept a breadth of five days journey as they advanced. Jornandes says that Arnegisclus fell at Marcianopolis, close to Varna near the shores of the Black sea. Marcellinus says the conflict took place on the banks of the Utus, which flows into the Danube a little to the east of Sophia, a place very far in the rear of Attila's advanced position, which Marcellinus himself states to have been at Thermopolis, supposed to mean Thermopylae. The probability is therefore, that the battle was fought near Marcianopolis. If it was fought near the Utus, Attila must have pursued his uninterrupted course afterwards through Macedonia and Thessaly. Theodosius in this dilemma attempted to tamper with the kings under Attila, and excited against him the princes of the Acatzires on the northern side of the Euxine. Attila is said to have been alarmed at this intelligence, and to have been fearful that the territory which he had ravaged to the south of the river, would be unable to support his immense army, and was induced by prudential motives to listen to the negotiators of Theodosius.

The immediate danger to the empire was averted by the conclusion of a truce, and Attila now turned his arms against the Acatzires, a Hunnish race dwelling on the borders of the Black sea, who were governed by a number of petty kings. Theodosius had offered them bribes, to induce them to withdraw from confederation with Attila. The messenger however, who was charged with the imperial presents, did not distribute them according to the estimated rank of the several princes, so that Curidach who was the senior king, received only the second present. Incensed at this, and considering himself to have been slighted and deprived of his due, he called in the aid of Attila against the other princes of the Acatzires. Attila without loss of time, sent a considerable force against them, slew some, and reduced the rest to subjection. He then invited Curidach to partake in the fruits of the victory, but he, suspecting some design against his person, and adroitly adapting his flattery to the pretensions which Attila had lately advanced, on the production of the divine sword, made answer, that it was a formidable thing for a man to come into the presence of a God; for if no one could steadfastly behold the face of the sun, how should he without injury look upon the greatest of divinities. By these means, Curidach retained his sovereignty, while the power of the rest was yielded up to the Hun.

27. Embassies to Constantinople to redemand the refugees.

Attila now sent ambassadors to Constantinople, to redemand the fugitives from his territory. He seems to have been at all times particularly irritable concerning those who withdrew themselves from subjection to his authority by flight to the Christians, and the certainty of their execution, if recaptured, rendered their protectors very unwilling to surrender them.

On this occasion his legates were received with great courtesy, and loaded with presents, but they were dismissed with assurances that there were no refugees at Constantinople. Four successive embassies were despatched to Theodosius, and enriched by the liberality of the Romans; for Attila, aware of the gifts by which his ambassadors were conciliated through fear of an abrupt infringement of the truce, whenever he wished to confer a benefit upon any of his favorites or dependants, found some excuse for sending them on a mission to enrich themselves.

The Romans obeyed him as their lord and master, and submitted to all his demands, not only dreading the renewal of hostilities by the Huns, but harassed by the warlike preparations of the Parthians, the maritime attacks of the Vandals in the Mediterranean, the inroads of the Isauri, and the repeated incursions of the Saracens who laid waste the eastern parts of the empire. They humbled themselves therefore towards Attila, and temporized with him, while they were preparing to make head against their other enemies, and levied troops, and made choice of generals to oppose them.

28. Edécon sent to Constantinople with Orestes. Chrysaphius. Maximin, Priscus, Bigilas. Agintheus.

In the following year (AD 448) Edécon, who is called a Scythian, a man highly distinguished by his military exploits, was sent to Constantinople by Attila, together with Orestes, who was of Roman extraction, dwelling in Paeonia near the Savus, which had been ceded to Attila by a treaty concluded with Aetius the commander of the forces of the Western empire.

Edécon proceeded to the imperial palace, and delivered the letters of Attila, in which he reiterated his complaints touching the fugitives, and threatened that he would have recourse to arms again, unless they were delivered up to him and the Romans desisted from ploughing the lands which he had lately wrested from them, or at least overrun. The territory which he claimed extended on the southern bank of the Danube, from Paeonia to the Thracian Novae, with a breadth of five days journey for an active man; and he forbad the Illyrian fair being held as heretofore on the banks of the Danube, but in Naissus which he had utterly destroyed, and now appointed to be the boundary between his states and the Romans. He demanded that the most distinguished men of consular dignity should be sent to his court to arrange all matters in dispute, and threatened, that if they should delay, he would advance to Sardica.

The letter having been read, Edécon delivered the message of his sovereign through the interpretation of Bigilas, and withdrew with him through another quarter of the royal palace, to visit Chrysaphius the shield-bearer of the emperor, who had then much influence. Edécon expressed great admiration at the splendor of the imperial residence, and, when they reached the apartment of Chrysaphius, Bigilas interpreted to him the words in which the Scythian had stated that he admired the magnificence and envied the wealth of the Romans. The eunuch seized this opportunity to tamper with the fidelity of the barbarian, and told him that he should enjoy like opulence and dwell under ceilings of gold, if he would exchange the party of the Scythians for that of the Romans. Edécon replied that it was not lawful for the servant of another master to do this without the permission of his lord; whereupon the insidious eunuch asked him if he had free access to Attila, and influence in the Hunnish court. Edécon replied that he was a confidential attendant, and took his turn with other chosen and distinguished individuals to watch in arms over his safety upon the days allotted to him. Thereupon Chrysaphius said, that if he would pledge himself to the Romans, he would promise him great advantages; but that leisure was necessary to make arrangements, for which purpose he proposed to him to return to supper without Orestes and the rest of the embassy.

Edécon having undertaken to do so, and having returned according to agreement, Bigilas acting as interpreter between them, they pledged their right hands and swore, the one that he would speak of things the most advantageous to Edécon, the other that he would not reveal their discourse, whether he might assent to the proposals or not. The eunuch, satisfied with this promise, proceeded to assure the Scythian that if on his return he would murder Attila and make his escape to the Romans he should enjoy great wealth and luxury. Edécon assented, but stated that money would be necessary to distribute amongst the soldiers under him, that they might assist him without reluctance, for which purpose he required fifty pounds weight of gold.

Chrysaphius would have disbursed the money immediately, but Edécon represented the necessity of his returning first to render an account of his embassy, and of his being accompanied by Bigilas who might bring Attila's answer concerning the refugees, and at the same time a communication from himself to state when and how the gold might be remitted to him; for that Attila would question him closely according to his custom, what gifts and how much money he had obtained from the Romans; nor should he be able to conceal the truth easily, on account of the numbers who were with him. Chrysaphius assented to this, and when his guest had withdrawn, he proceeded to disclose the treacherous scheme to the emperor, who immediately sent for Martialius, the master or warden of the palace, to whom by virtue of his office all the counsels of the emperor were necessarily confided, as he had the superintendence of the letter-carriers, the interpreters, and the soldiers who kept guard in the palace.

It seemed good to the emperor and these his advisers to send Maximin with Bigilas under the existing circumstances, to the court of Attila: that Bigilas in the character of interpreter should obey the instructions he might receive from Edécon, but that Maximin should have charge to deliver the letter of the emperor, remaining entirely ignorant of the infamous conspiracy which was to be carried on under the cover of his mission. Theodosius wrote in the credentials of the ambassadors that Bigilas was the interpreter, but that Maximin was a man of much greater distinction and very much in his confidence. He exhorted Attila not to infringe the treaty, inasmuch as he then sent to him seventeen refugees in addition to those who had been already delivered up, and assured him that there were no more in his dominions. Maximin was instructed to use his endeavours to persuade Attila not to require an ambassador of higher rank, as it had been customary for his ancestors and the other kings of Scythia, to receive any military or civil envoy; and suggest the expediency of his sending Onegesius to arrange the matters which were under discussion; and represent the impracticability of Attila's conferring with a man of consular dignity at Sardica which had been demolished by the Huns.

Maximin persuaded the sophist and historian Priscus to accompany him on this expedition; and if the eight books which he afterwards wrote had not unfortunately perished, those extracts only being preserved which relate to the embassies, we should not have to lament the insufficiency of our materials for some parts of the history of Attila.

They set forth therefore in company with the barbarians, and proceeded to Sardica, thirteen days journey from Constantinople. Here they tarried, and thought it advisable to invite Edécon and his companions to take their meal with them. The natives furnished them with sheep and oxen, which they slaughtered and prepared for their repast. During the banquet the barbarians exalted the name of Attila, and the Greeks that of the emperor, whereupon Bigilas said that it was not just to compare a God with a man, intimating thereby that Theodosius was the divinity and Attila a human potentate. The guests took great offence at the insinuation, and grew very warm on the subject, but the ambassadors exerted themselves to change the subject and pacify them, and after the supper Maximin presented Edécon and Orestes with silken apparel and oriental jewels. Orestes outstand Edécon, and observed after his departure to Maximin, that he acted well and wisely in not imitating the conduct of those about the emperor; for some had invited to supper Edécon alone, and had loaded him with gifts; but the ambassadors, not being aware of the circumstance to which he alluded, asked him in what respect he had been neglected and Edécon honored, to which he made no reply, but withdrew.

The subject being discussed in conversation the next day, Bigilas observed that Orestes ought not to have expected to receive the same honors as Edécon, inasmuch as Orestes was the follower and scribe of Attila, but Edécon was very distinguished in warfare, and being of Hunnish blood was in higher estimation; after which he addressed Edécon in his own language, and subsequently informed the ambassadors, that he had told him what had been said by Orestes, and with difficulty had allayed his anger on the subject, but the historian does not rely implicitly on the veracity of the interpretation.

Arriving at Naissus five days journey from the Danube, they found it demolished by the Huns, but some sick persons were abiding in the ruins of the temples. The party sought for a clear place to unyoke their beasts of burden, for the whole bank of the river was strewn with the bones of those who had fallen in the war; an incident which furnishes a horrible picture of the desolating atrocity of Hunnish warfare, by which the whole population of a distinguished town had been exterminated, and as yet after the lapse of several years, there had been none to bury their remains.

On the following day they visited Agintheus who commanded the forces in Illyria, and had his quarters not far from Naissus, that they might deliver to him the injunctions of the emperor, and receive from his hands five refugees who were to make up the complement of seventeen, concerning whom he had written to Attila, and who were to be delivered up to his relentless indignation. Agintheus, as he was ordered, surrendered the ill-fated fugitives, softening the harshness of the act towards them by the expression of his unavailing regret.

29. Cross the Danube, and reach the tents of Attila

On the succeeding day they continued their journey from the mountains of Naissus towards the Danube, passing through some woody and circuitous defiles, so that those who were unacquainted with the country and imagined they were travelling westward, were astonished in the morning at seeing the sunrise opposite to them, and fancied it was a prodigy portending the subversion of all established order, till it was explained to them that on account of natural impediments, that part of the road was necessarily turned towards the east.

From the mountainous passes they issued into a level and woody district, where barbarian ferrymen received the whole party into canoes which they had themselves scooped out of solid stems, and conveyed them across the Danube. It seems that they had travelled night and day, excepting when they halted at Sardica, at Naissus, and after the interview with Agintheus. The boats had not been prepared for the ambassadors, but to ferry over the river a multitude of Attila's people, whom they met on the way, for Attila had made a pretence of desiring to hunt in the territories wrested from the Romans, though in fact it was a preparation for war, which he meditated under the pretext that all the refugees had not been delivered up to him.

Having crossed the Danube, and proceeded about 70 stadia or a little more than eight English miles, they were made to halt on a plain, while the attendants of Edécon carried the news of their arrival to Attila. In the evening, while they were at supper, two Scythians arrived at their quarters, and ordered them to proceed to Attila, but having been requested to alight from their horses, they partook of the meal, and on the following morning served as their conductors. About the ninth hour of the day they reached the numerous tents of Attila, and being about to pitch their own on a knoll, the barbarians forbad it, because those of Attila were on the level ground.

The Romans having therefore established themselves where they were directed, Edécon, Orestes, Scottas, and others of the principal men, intruded themselves, and began to make enquiries into the objects of the embassy. At first the Romans looked at each other with surprise and gave no answer to the unbecoming questions, but the barbarians were troublesome and urgent in the enquiries, whereupon they were told that the message of the emperor was unto Attila, and no other person. Scottas answered angrily that they were sent by their leader to make this enquiry, and had not come to gratify their own curiosity. The Romans represented that it was nowhere customary for ambassadors without entering into the presence of the person to whom they had been sent to be called upon to declare the objects of their mission through the intervention of other persons; that the Scythians who had been on missions to the emperor well knew this, and that, unless admitted into the presence, as the ambassadors of Attila had always been, they would not communicate their instructions.

The messengers of Attila returned to him, and soon after coming back without Edécon, declared to the Romans all the particulars concerning which they were sent to treat by the emperor, and ordered them, if they had nothing further to communicate, to take their departure as speedily as possible.

The Romans were amazed, and, being unable to conjecture through what channel the secrets of the emperor had been divulged, thought it prudent to decline giving any answer, unless admitted to the royal presence; whereupon they were ordered to depart instantly. While they were preparing for the journey, Bigilas blamed them for the answer they had given, saying that it would be better to be detected in a falsehood, than to return without accomplishing their purpose; and asserted that if he could have come to the sight of Attila, he should easily have persuaded him to recede from his dispute with the Romans, having become well acquainted with him, when he had accompanied the mission of Anatolius; whence Edécon was also well disposed towards him; so that, under pretext of the embassy, by speaking truth or falsehood, as occasion might require, they might complete the arrangements touching the conspiracy against Attila, and the transmission of the gold which Edécon had stated to be necessary, that it might be divided amongst the satellites: but he little suspected, that he had been betrayed, for Edécon, whether his promises, as is most probable, had been deceitful from the first, or he had taken alarm, lest Orestes, indignant at what had passed at Sardica, should report to Attila that he had had separate and private conferences with the emperor and Chrysaphius, had divulged the whole conspiracy to the Hun, both the quota of gold that had been required, and the points concerning which the Romans had been instructed to negotiate.

The orders of Attila had been peremptory, and although it was night, the ambassadors, hungry and cold, were under the necessity of making ready for their departure, when a second message from the great king enjoined them to tarry till a more seasonable hour; and at the same time he sent them an ox and some river fish, on which they supped and retired to rest, hoping that he might be more favorably disposed on the morrow; but in the morning the same messengers returned, ordering them to depart, if they had nothing else to communicate.

They prepared therefore once more for the journey, notwithstanding the earnest suggestion of Bigilas, that they should answer that they had other things to set forth. The historian Priscus, through friendship to Maximin, who appeared very much dejected at the disgraceful issue of his mission, taking with him Rusticius, who understood the Hunnish language, for an interpreter, went to Scottas, and promised him ample presents from Maximin, if he would obtain for him an interview with Attila; assuring him that the subject matter of the embassy was not only important to the two nations, but personally to his brother Onegesius who was then absent from the court; and he adroitly added, that he understood he had great weight with Attila, but that he should better know how to estimate his importance, if he could prevail in this point. Scottas replied, that he had quite as much influence as Onegesius, and would prove it; and he mounted his horse immediately, and rode to the tent of the monarch. Priscus returning to Maximin found him and Bigilas lying on the grass, and, having declared what he had done, and recommended to Maximin to look out the gifts for Scottas and consider what he should say to Attila, was much applauded, and those amongst the retinue, who were actually starting, were called back, and their departure was suspended till the result of the application of Scottas should be known. While they were thus employed, they were summoned by Scottas to the presence of Attila.

Entering they beheld the monarch seated on a wooden throne, and guarded by a numerous circle of barbarians. Maximin alone approaching saluted him, while the rest of the Romans stood aloof; and, having delivered the letter of Theodosius, he said that the emperor prayed for the health and prosperity of him and his people. Attila answered, "May it be to the Romans, as they wish to me", and immediately turning his discourse to Bigilas, he called him a shameless beast, and asked how he presumed to come before him, knowing what terms of peace had been concluded between himself and Anatolius, and that no ambassadors should have been sent to him before all the refugees had been delivered up. Bigilas having replied, that there was no refugee of Scythian blood remaining in the empire, for that all had been given up, he waxed more angry, and exclaimed with loudness and violence, that he would crucify him, and give him for food to the birds, if he were not scrupulous of infringing the laws concerning ambassadors by awarding to him the just punishment of his impudence, and the rashness of his speech; for that many refugees were still amongst the Romans, whose names he ordered the secretaries to read from a tablet. After that had been performed, he commanded him to depart immediately, and Eslas to accompany him and bear a message to the Romans, that every fugitive, since the time when Carpileo the son of Aetius had been sent to Attila as a hostage from the Western empire, must be forthwith delivered up; inasmuch as he would not suffer his own servants to bear arms against him, however little they could avail for the protection of the Romans: "for", he added, using nearly the language of Sennacherib, "which of all the cities or fortresses that I have thought fit to capture, has been successfully defended against me?" He further directed them after having delivered his message concerning the fugitives, to return and inform him whether the Romans chose to surrender them, or to await the war which he should wage against them; but he commanded Maximin to stay for his answer to the letter of Theodosius, and enquired for the presents of the emperor, which were given to him. The ambassadors retired to their tents, where Bigilas expressed his surprise at the violent demeanor of Attila towards him, who had been formerly received with so much gentleness. The Romans imagined that the conversation at Sardica, in which Bigilas had called him a mortal and Theodosius a divinity, must have been related to him by some of the guests, who were present at that banquet; but Bigilas, who had intimate acquaintance with the Hunnish court, would not credit the suggestion, saying that no one excepting Edécon would dare to enter into discourse with him on such matters, and that he would undoubtedly be silent, not merely on account of his oath, but through fear that he might be condemned to death for having been present at, and lent himself to, secret counsels against the life of his sovereign.

While these matters were under discussion, Edécon returned, and, drawing Bigilas aside, renewed the subject of the gold which he required for distribution, and, after giving directions concerning its payment, he withdrew. Priscus, the friend of Maximin, who was kept in ignorance of the atrocious conspiracy, having enquired into the subject of that conversation, Bigilas who was himself deceived by Edécon, eluded the enquiry by saying that Edécon had complained that he was brought into trouble on account of the detention of the fugitives, and that all of them should have been delivered up, or ambassadors of the highest dignity sent for the purpose of pacifying Attila.

A further command was presently issued by the monarch, that neither Bigilas nor any of the Romans should buy any Roman captive or barbarian slave, or any horse or other article except necessary provender, until the differences should be adjusted; and this he did with subtlety, that Bigilas might have no excuse for bringing the gold which was promised to Edécon; and, under pretence of writing an answer to Theodosius, he required the Romans to await the return home of Onegesius, that they might deliver to him the presents sent by the emperor.

Onegesius was at that time absent, having been sent to establish the eldest son of Attila and Creca on the throne of the Acatares, whose reduction has been already mentioned. Bigilas was therefore despatched alone with Eslas to bring back the answer concerning the refugees, but in truth to afford him an opportunity of fetching the gold, and the rest were detained in their tents, but after one day's interval they were made to proceed together with Attila towards the north of Hungary.

30. Proceed northward. Attila marries Eskam.

The ambassadors had not travelled far in the suite of the Hunnish monarch, when their conductors directed them to follow a different road, for Attila thought fit to tarry in a certain hamlet, where he had determined to add his daughter Eskam to the number of his wives. We are informed by Priscus that this marriage was conformable to the law of the Scythians. His expression is somewhat remarkable, and literally rendered is, "where he purposed to marry his daughter Eskam, having indeed many wives, but espousing this one also according to Scythian law". Some writers have taken occasion from this passage to assert that there was no prohibition amongst the Huns to any marriage, however repugnant to propriety on account of relationship, and St. Jerome has made a similar declaration, probably with no better foundation, concerning the Persians, amongst whom incest was no more generally permitted, than polygamy was amongst the Jews. The instances of two wives recorded in the case of Lamech, and of Jacob, and Elkanah, are evidently particular cases departing from the established practice, and the permission given to the kings of the Jews to possess many wives and concubines, was the consequence of the Lord's having conceded to the Jews, as a punishment for their perverse entreaties, "a king over them, that they might be like all the nations"; a king therefore having all the privileges enjoyed by the adjoining potentates, namely that they could do no wrong and might take any number of wives, however nearly related to them in blood, notwithstanding the prohibition that had been given prospectively concerning them, that they should not multiply their wives, a prohibition which was certainly respected by the generality of the Jews.

The words of Priscus do not imply that either polygamy or incest were lawful to all the Huns, but that it was lawful to Attila, as it had been to Cambyses, on account of his prerogative. The Hungarian writers, indignant at the reproaches cast on the morals of their supposed ancestors on this occasion, have attempted to make it appear that the lady espoused by Attila was not his child, but the daughter of a man named Eskam, considering the undeclined name Eskam to be a genitive case, and rendering the preceding word the daughter of instead of his daughter. On a careful consideration of the construction of sentences in the Greek written by Priscus and others of that period, it will be apparent that the words cannot mean to marry the daughter of Eskam.

31. Storm, and village where dwelt a widow of Bleda

While Attila was reveling with his new bride, the ambassadors were conducted onward across a level country, and traversed several rivers in canoes or boats used by the people who lived on their banks, similar to those in which they had crossed the Danube. The next in size to that river were stated to have been the Drecon, the Ugas, and Tiphesas, which last is the Teiss, but it has not been found practicable to identify the two others. The lesser streams were passed in boats that were carried on wagons by the barbarians through the country which was liable to be flooded.

Millet was brought to the Romans for food from the villages instead of wheat, and mead instead of wine, together with a sort of beer made from barley which was called by the natives cam. After a long and weary journey, they pitched their tents at evening near a lake of clear water which the inhabitants of a neighboring hamlet were in the habit of fetching for drink.

A violent storm of wind and rain with exceedingly vivid lightning came on immediately after they had encamped, and not only overset their tents and laid all flat, but washed away their provisions and furniture into the lake. The Romans were so terrified, that they fled in various directions, floundering through the tempest in the dark night, to avoid the same fate as their chattels, till they fortunately met again in the village hard by, where they were very clamorous to be supplied with everything they wanted. The Scythian cottagers ran out of their hovels and inquired into the cause of their vociferations, and being informed by the barbarians who were in company that they had been put to confusion by the storm, they invited them in, and kindled speedily a cheerful blaze with dry reeds.

The mistress of the hamlet was a lady, who had been one of the wives of Bleda, and hearing of the misadventure of the Romans, she sent to them a present of victuals, and also paid them the singular compliment, which however was a usual practice of honorable hospitality amongst the Huns, of sending them some beautiful Scythian women, who were enjoined to comply with all their wishes; but the ambassadors were either too decorous or too disheartened to be desirous of availing themselves of the offer, and declined the favors which were destined for them. The ladies were regaled with a portion of the supper and dismissed, and the ambassadors, having taken their repose in the cottages of the natives, proceeded at daybreak in search of their equipments, part of which they found on the spot where they had encamped, part on the banks of the lake, and part in the water; but the whole of their goods was recovered, and they tarried all day in the hamlet to dry them in the sun, which shone out brilliantly after that stormy night. When due attention had been paid to the beasts of burden, they proceeded to visit the queen, and, having saluted her, they returned thanks for her hospitality, and presented her with three silver vessels, some crimson fleeces, Indian pepper, dates, and other articles for desert, which not being found amongst the barbarians were valuable to them.

Having thus returned her compliment, they took their leave and proceeded on their journey for seven days, till the Scythian conductors made them halt in a village on their way, because Attila was coming in that direction, and it was not allowable for them to travel before him. At this place they fell in with ambassadors from the Western empire, Count Romulus, Primutus praefect of Noricum, and Romanus general of a division. Constantius was with them, whom Aetius had sent as a secretary to Attila, and Tatullus the father of Orestes who was with Edécon, not being members of the legation, but having undertaken the journey through private motives, the former on account of his previous intimacy with them in Italy, the latter from relationship, his son Orestes having married the daughter of Romulus from the city Patavion in Noricum. Their object was to pacify Attila, who required that Silvanus, a Roman silversmith, should be delivered up to him, because he had received some golden vessels from another Constantius, a native of Western Gaul, who had also been sent as a secretary by Aetius to Attila and Bleda. When the Huns were laying siege to Sirmium in Paeonia, those vessels had been delivered to Constantius by the bishop of the place for his own ransom in case he should survive the capture of the city, and to redeem others amongst the captives if he should have fallen; but Constantius after the taking of Sirmium was faithless to his trust, and pawned the vessels for money to Silvanus, to be redeemed within a given time, or the sale of them to stand good.

Attila and Bleda, having suspected this Constantius of treason, crucified him, and Attila, hearing what had been done concerning the golden vessels, demanded Silvanus to be given up, as a robber of his property. The object of the embassy was therefore to persuade Attila that Silvanus was no thief, but that having taken the goods in pawn from Constantius, he had sold them as unredeemed pledges to the first priests who wished for them, because it was not lawful to sell them for the use of laymen, as they had been consecrated. The ambassadors were directed to try to prevail upon Attila to give up his claim to the vessels for this reason, and, if he persevered, to offer him gold in their stead, but on no account to give up the innocent silversmith to be crucified. The two parties of Eastern and Western Romans followed the route of Attila, and, after crossing some more rivers, they arrived at a large village, where Attila had a fixed residence.

32. Situation of the residence of Attila.

It is not possible to gather, from the statement of the journey of the ambassadors, the exact situation of this place, but the number of days they had travelled makes it evident that it must have been in the north of Hungary. They had not however arrived at the Carpathian mountains. Tokay has been mentioned by Buat as the most probable site. It has been also conjectured that the tents of Attila, which were first visited by the legation, were pitched opposite Viddin, and that Jasberin was the site of the royal village; but other writers have been of opinion that it was in that part of Moldavia which produces neither stone nor wood, for Priscus states that there was none in the neighborhood, and that the stone, with which the baths of Onegesius were built, was brought out of the land of the Paeonians. That they did not cross the Danube near Viddin is however evident, because it lies north-east of Nissa, and Priscus says their general course was westward of that place; and it seems that they must have crossed a little below Belgrade, and passed the Themes, the Bega, and the Theiss in the first instance, and afterwards the large tributary rivers which fall into the Theiss from the westward, and shaped their course towards Tokay. Jornandes calls the three rivers named by Priscus, the Tysia, Tibiscia, and Dricca. Tibiscus is the known name of the Theiss, and Tysia is probably a river falling into the Theiss which may have given to it the modern name. Nothing is known concerning the Dricca. To have reached Moldavia they must have traversed the rivers of Wallachia, shaping their course eastward after visiting the tents of Attila; but the only certain fact is that they did cross the Theiss, which lay in the contrary direction, and having done so they could only have reached Moldavia by recrossing that river, and threading one of the three passes through the mountains that separate it from Transylvania, neither of which suppositions is consistent with the narrative of Priscus. In another passage that writer states that the land of the Paeonians was by the river Saus, and it is certain from two passages in Menander, that Saus was the Saave, which falls into the Danube from the opposite side a little below the Theiss, and the land in question was evidently the modern Sirmia near Belgrade, whence the stone might easily be carried up the river Theiss to Tokay in boats, but could not with any degree of probability have been conveyed to Moldavia. The facility of water-carriage probably induced Onegesius to procure the stone from Sirmia, for although there might be stone nearer in the mountains to the north, the conveyance of it would have been more difficult, and the Huns were probably from their habits impatient of labor in the quarries.

33. Hrings of Avares or Huns which were destroyed by Pepin under Charlemagne.

In the same situation, or not far distant, on the right of the Theiss, was the strong hold and palace of the king of the Avar Huns, which was called the Hring and was destroyed by the armies of Charlemagne in 796, and is said by the writers of that period to have subsisted many centuries. These stupendous works are mentioned by Jornandes, who says they were called Hunniwar by the Huns, but he does not describe them; and it is observable that the name of Ring by which they were known in the eighth century is also a Teutonic word, which probably had descended from the Huns of Attila, to the Avars who then occupied them. Priscus uses an expression equivalent to ring, when he speaks of the enclosure, which surrounded the dwelling of Attila, by the Greek word peribolos. In the reign of Charlemagne, we find the marvelous fortifications of the Huns occupied by the Avars, who acquired the ascendancy at a period subsequent to the death of Attila, by whom they had been subdued, and afterwards were called Huns by the neighboring nations.

These works are particularly described by Notgerus Balbus, commonly called the Monk of St. Gall in a passage of most difficult construction. He states, that the land of the Huns was surrounded by nine circles; and that when, imagining the circles to be common hedges, he asked Aldabert, who had served under Charlemagne, what was the wonder, he learned from him that one circle was as wide, or comprehended in itself as much, as the distance from Constance to a place called Castrum Turonicum, of which the site in all probability cannot now be ascertained.

The abbot of Saint Gall was under the jurisdiction of the bishop of Constance, and Castrum Turonicum must have been some place in that neighborhood not having a see. It does not mean Tours, which was Caesarodunum Turonum. He goes on to state, that each circle was so constructed with stems of oak, beech, and fir, that it was twenty feet wide and twenty high; that the whole cavity was filled with hard stones, or tenacious chalk, perhaps meaning mortar. The surface was covered with sods. Between, bushes were planted, which (according to the probable meaning of the expression) were cut after the manner of clipped hedges. Between these circles, hamlets and villages were so placed, that the human voice could be heard from one to another. Opposite these buildings, narrow doors were fabricated in the strong walls. "Also (he adds) from the second circle, which was constructed in like manner as the first, there was an extent of twenty Teutonic, which are forty Italian, miles unto the third. In like manner even unto the ninth; although the circles themselves were much more contracted one than another; and from circle to circle tenements and habitations were so arranged in every direction, that by the sound of trumpets the signification of everything could be comprehended at the distance between each of them".

From the very obscure passage of which the above is a close translation, we learn first that the distance between the two outer circles was equal to that of Constance from an unknown town; that the distance between the second and third was forty Italian miles of five thousand feet, equal to near thirty-eight English miles. The word also might seem to imply that the distance between the first and second circle, or between Constance and Castrum Turonicum, was also about thirty-eight English miles, but that would give too great a diameter. It is much more difficult to explain what follows; it may imply that the spaces between the circles were invariably equal, adding the mere truism, that the circumference of the inner concentric circles was necessarily smaller than that of the outer; or it may imply that the walls were built in the same manner throughout, but that the inner spaces were narrower. If the former interpretation be adopted, which certainly appears more conformable to the words, and the spaces between the several rings, and between the inner ring and the centre be considered to have been similar, that is, thirty-eight English miles, the diameter of the outer circle would be six hundred and eighty-four miles, and would enclose a great deal more than the whole of Hungary, and is inconsistent with what we have reason to believe, that the rings were situated between the Danube and the Theiss.

A circle of about one hundred and fifty miles diameter will enclose the greater part of Upper Hungary between those two rivers, the Mora, and the Krapac mountains, and such was probably the site and extent of those great works, supposing the space between the two exterior belts to have been less than between the second and third, perhaps sixteen miles, and the remaining twenty-one miles of the radius, or forty-two of the diameter, to have been divided amongst the seven interior. The inner portion would thus have consisted of seven concentric circles, like the town of Ecbatana, as described by Herodotus, to which two wider belts were superadded. The celebrated labyrinth of Crete was perhaps a structure of the same kind.

Eginhart, notary of Charlemagne, in his Annales, says that in 791 the emperor defeated the Huns upon the Danube, drove them from their fortifications, and penetrated to the mouth of the river Arrabon or Raab. That in 796 Eric duke of Friuli plundered the Ringus, and that later in the same year, Pepin having driven the Huns across the Theiss, and utterly demolished their palace, "which is Ringus, but is called by the Lombards Campus", sent their treasures to Charlemagne. In his Vita Caroli Magni, the notary says the wars with the Huns lasted eight years, and were so bloody that all the dwellings in Pannonia were destroyed, and not a vestige of a human habitation remained in the place where the palace of the chagawn had been situated.

The anonymous annals of Charlemagne say that in 791 he took the defenses of the Avars, advanced to the Raab, and retired; and in 796 he received a message in Saxony, which informed him that Pepin was lodged with his army in the Ring. The unknown author of another Vita Caroli Magni, says that in 791 the Huns abandoned their works near the Danube, and he marched to the river Raab. In 796 Henry duke of Friuli (for Henry and Eric are different forms of the same name) having sent a force into Pannonia, plundered the Ring of the Avars, who were divided by civil war, the chagawn having been murdered by his own people; and he sent their treasures, which had been accumulated there during a long course of centuries, to Charlemagne. That in the same year Thudun came over to him with a great part of the Avars, and was baptized; and before the end of that year (796) a message was received by Charlemagne, that Pepin had come to blows with the new chagawn and his nobles, and again a second message that Pepin was lodged in the Ring.

Another author who wrote about the year 858, says that in 796 Pepin arrived at the celebrated place which is called Rinch, where the Huns surrendered to him. An ancient Saxon poet, who wrote in the reign of Arnolf, AD 888, gives a similar account, and says that Pepin beat the Huns beyond the Theiss, and leveled to the ground their royal residence called Hring. It is quite clear that the palace or royal residence in which the plunder of Europe had been then stored up for three or four centuries was the central ring or circle of the nine circumvallations which have been described; and, as they had existed for centuries, there is no reason to doubt that they were the identical fortifications which Jornandes states to have existed in the time of Attila under the name of Hunniwar. The central ring was perhaps in the neighborhood of Gomor in Upper Hungary. It is observable that Eusebius, speaking of the six concentric walls to the Babylon of Nebuchodonosor, calls them by the same word (periboloi) which is used by Priscus in describing the residence of Attila.

A passage concerning the abode of the Hunnish monarch in Saemund's Edda, which has been entirely misunderstood by the Latin translator, and which the annotator calls one of the passages in the poem which cannot be solved, alludes to the concentric circumvallations as having existed in the time of Attila, and it was only difficult, because he knew not the nature of the defenses to which it refers. It may be translated literally thus. "They saw the land of Attila and deep towers; the fierce men stand in that high bourg, the hall around the people of the South, surrounded with set-beams, with circles bound together, with white shields, the obstacle of spearmen. There Attila was drinking wine in his divine hall. The warders sat without." The translator renders the word sess-meithom, seat-beams, and explains it thus, that the hall had wooden seats round it, and that either a bundle of shields was hung over head above the seats, or single shields tied together suspended against the wall. On reference to the detailed account of the Hunnish fortifications, it is evident that the set-beams are the stems (stipites) with which the circumvallations were constructed; that the circles bound together are the concentric belts or rings; that the white shields are a figurative illustration of the same, white, because as the Monk of St. Gall says, they were made with chalk, and shields, as explained in the next line, because they were obstacles opposed to the attack of an enemy.

The editors could not have found this easy solution of the passage in Scandinavian literature, and they looked no further. The conformity of these various and very ancient authorities gives strong reason for assuming that Attila had (to use the remarkable expression of Ammianus Marcellinus when speaking of the circular positions of the Alans) circumcircated the district of Upper Hungary, and that hither Priscus was conducted; not to the inmost ring, but the village situated perhaps on the outside of its eastern entrance near Tokay, as Sicambria the favorite abode of Attila near Buda was perhaps at its southern entrance; but it is possible that the exterior belts may not have been constructed till a later period. The dwelling of Attila, and that of Onegesius, are both described by Priscus, as being surrounded with a circular construction of wood, which he calls peribolos, not for security, but for ornament, which shows the affection the Huns had for the Ring in their architecture. The palace of Attila exceeded all the other structures in size and conspicuous appearance. It was built with massive timber, and beautifully polished planks, and adorned with towers. The dwelling of Onegesius was the next in importance, but not ornamented with towers, though in like manner environed by a wooden ring, formed of upright timber close set in the ground. At a short distance were the baths which Onegesius, who had great wealth and influence amongst the Huns, had caused to be constructed of stone from the Sirmian quarries, by a captive architect who was a native of Sirmium, and had vainly hoped that his manumission would be the reward of his labors; but Onegesius, after the building was completed, made the unfortunate architect superintendant of the bath, and caused him to wait upon himself and his friends during their ablutions.

34. Observations of a Hun on the state of the empire.

As Attila made his entry into this village, a number of damsels advanced to meet him, arranged in ranks under, white veils of exceeding fineness, which were of great length, and so extended and held aloft by the hands of the women, that under every one of them walked seven or more damsels, singing Scythian airs, and the rows of young women thus placed under the veils were very numerous.

The way to the royal residence lay by the dwelling of Onegesius, and, as Attila was passing it, the wife of Onegesius came out with a multitude of servants bearing dressed fish and wine, which is the highest compliment amongst the Huns, and she saluted Attila praying him to partake of her liberality. He, wishing to appear gracious to the wife of his confidential friend, ate as he sat upon his horse, a table of massive silver being lifted up to him by the attendants; and, having tasted of the cup offered to him, he retired into his own palace, which was placed in a more elevated situation than the other buildings, and overlooked them.

The ambassadors were invited into the house of Onegesius, who had returned together with the son of Attila, and they dined there, being received by the wife of Onegesius and the most distinguished of his relatives; for he had not leisure to partake with them, having been summoned to make a report of the transactions of his mission to Attila, who had not before seen him since his return, and to detail die particulars of the misadventure of Attila's son, who had broken his right arm by a fall. When they withdrew from the hospitable board of Onegesius, the Romans pitched their tents in the neighborhood of the palace of Attila, that Maximin might be at hand to confer with him or his counselors. Early the next morning Priscus was sent by Maximin to Onegesius to present to him the gifts which he brought on his own part and that of the emperor, and to learn whether the favorite would grant him an interview, and at what time.

The Huns had not risen so early as the Romans, and, the doors being all closed, the historian remained with the menials who bore the presents, waiting without the ring of timber that surrounded the buildings, until some person should happen to come out. While he was walking up and down to beguile the time, he was surprised on being addressed by a man habited as a Hun who bade him hail in the Greek language, which was rarely spoken by any amongst them, except captives from Thrace or the coast of Illyria, and those might be at once recognized by the miserable and squalid condition of their garments and hair; but this man appeared to be a Scythian in excellent plight, with his hair neatly cropped all round.

Having returned his salutation, Priscus was informed that he was a Greek who had gone to attend the fair at the Mysian city Viminacium on the Danube, where he had married a rich wife and established himself; but, on the capture of that town by the Huns, he and all his wealth had fallen to the lot of Onegesius, in the division of the spoil amongst the principal followers of Attila. Sometime after, having fought valiantly in company with the Huns against the Romans and Acatzires, according to the Scythian law he had regained his liberty by surrendering to his master all the plunder he had made in the war; and, having a place at the table of Onegesius, he was well satisfied with his present condition: for that the Huns, when the labors of warfare were at an end, lived without any cares, enjoying their possessions without any molestation, and in perfect security. On the other hand he drew a melancholy picture of the state of the empire, of which the subjects were easily taken or slain in war, because the jealousy of their masters prevented their being entrusted with arms for their own defence, and that even those, who carried arms on behalf of the Romans, suffered grievously from the incapacity and inertness of their officers; but that in peace the case was even worse than in war, through the weight of taxes and the extortion of evil men in power, the laws not being equally administered to all, but transgressed with impunity by the rich and powerful, while strictly carried into operation against the indigent, if indeed they survived the period of a protracted and ruinous lawsuit; and so deeply rooted was the corruption of justice, that no man amongst them could hope for the protection of the laws, without conciliating by money the favor of the judge and his dependants.

The historian according to his own account attempted to reply to the censures of the apostate Greek by a feeble panegyric on the system of Roman jurisprudence, without contradicting the facts that were alleged. This brought forth a brief observation, which appears to have been unanswerable and uncontroverted, that the constitution of Rome might be good, and her laws excellent, but that both were perverted by the corruption of those who administered them.

35. Onegesius. Kreka. Extent of Attila's power in the North,

extending to the confines of the Medes.

The door having been at length opened accidentally, Priscus eagerly enquired for Onegesius, stating that he came from Maximin the ambassador of the Romans; but this application did not procure admission for him, and he was requested to wait till the Hun should come forth. Onegesius having appeared soon after, accepted the gold and presents, which he ordered his attendants to carry into the house; and he replied to the request which Maximin made for an interview, that he would visit the Roman in his tent. This he did soon after, and, having thanked him for the presents, enquired upon what account he had requested an interview.

Maximin expressed an earnest desire that Onegesius should personally proceed into the Roman territory, and enquire into and adjust the points in dispute favorably to the emperor. Onegesius rejected with indignation all tampering with his allegiance, asking if they imagined that he did not esteem servitude under Attila to be more honorable than independent wealth amongst the Romans; but added that he could be more useful to them by remaining where he was and softening the frequent irritation of his monarch, than by going amongst them and exposing himself to blame, if he should act in any respect against the opinion of Attila.

Before he departed, Onegesius consented to receive the future communications of the ambassador through the intervention of Priscus, because the high dignity of Maximin would have rendered frequent and protracted interviews with him unbecoming and probably liable to suspicion. On the following day the historian penetrated the ring which enclosed the mansions of Attila, being the bearer of presents to Kreka (or Creca) his principal queen, who had borne him three sons, of whom the eldest had been raised to the rank of king over the Acatzires and other tribes bordering upon the Euxine. The various buildings within the enclosure were of wood; some constructed with planks expertly fitted together and beautified with pannels or carvings of insculpture; others of straight massive timber perfectly squared and planed, and ornamented in relief with highly wrought beams or mouldings.

The visitors having been admitted by the Huns, who were standing at the door, found the queen reclining upon a soft counterpane, the floor of the room being delicately carpeted, and opposite to her were sitting upon the carpet damsels employed in embroidering veils or scarfs, which were worn by the Huns over their clothing for ornament. Having saluted her and presented the gifts, Priscus withdrew, and, waiting for Onegesius who was known to have entered the residence of Attila, he proceeded towards some of the other buildings, in which he then resided, without any interruption from the guards to whom he was known. Standing amidst the crowd of people, he observed the multitude in motion, and a press and noise, as if the monarch was coming forth; and presently he saw him, accompanied by Onegesius, issue from his dwelling, bearing himself haughtily and casting his eyes round on all sides.

Many, who had controversies, came before him, and received in the open air his sentence on the points in dispute; and, after the close of his judicial labors, he re-entered the house and gave audience to the ambassadors of various barbarian nations. Priscus continued to await the leisure of Onegesius in the palace court, where he was accosted by the ambassadors from the Western empire, who inquired whether Maximin had received his dismissal, or was under the necessity of remaining.

Priscus replied that he was waiting for Onegesius to ascertain that very point, and enquired into the success of their mission, but was informed by them that Attila was quite inexorable and denounced immediate war against Valentinian, unless either Silvanus or the golden vessels were delivered up to him. Priscus, having expressed his surprise at the arrogance of Attila, received some interesting information from Romulus, whose sources of knowledge were undeniable, his daughter being married to Orestes the follower of Edécon and scribe of Attila, whose father Tatullus was even then in the company.

This information is very important, for we may rely upon it as the true statement of the power of Attila at that time, and the extent of his empire. He asserted that no king, either of Scythia or any other land had done such great things in so short a time; inasmuch as his rule extended over the islands in the ocean, and in addition to all Scythia, he had reduced the Romans to be tributary to him; and that, not content with his European conquests, he was meditating even then the subjugation of Persia.

The Danish historians, who are determined to shut their eyes against the fact, that Attila was master of the Danish islands and the south of Scandinavia which the Romans considered to be an island called by them Thule, and that in truth they have no authentic history previous to the time of Attila, who is mixed up under diverse names in their ancient legends, have asserted that Russia was looked upon as insular by the Romans, and was meant by the islands of the ocean upon this occasion.

But the statement of Priscus is an unequivocal admission by an enemy to Attila, who had the means of knowing and could not be mistaken, that he did rule over the islands of the ocean generally, and whether part of Russia was supposed to be an island and included under the denomination or not, that single portion could not by any interpretation have been intended to the exclusion of the rest. On the other hand the words may be interpreted to include Great Britain and Ireland, and it may be a matter of doubt whether even that was not intended, and whether, although Attila never set foot in Great Britain, the legends of St Patric and Arthur, which are contemporaneous with and have evident reference to him, do not represent the influence and authority which he had acquired in the British isles through his emissaries and the weight of his Antichristian pretensions; but with respect to his dominion over the Danish and Scandinavian territory, which was more particularly called the islands of the ocean, the assertion of Romulus made in the presence of the father of Orestes would have been irrefragable, even if it had not been confirmed, as it is, by the concurring evidence of the Scandinavian sagas and Teutonic legends.

The Eastern Romans, having enquired through what quarter he would be able to attack the Persians, were further informed by him that the dominions of Attila extended to the neighborhood of the Medes, and that Bazic and Cursic, two Huns of the blood royal, who ruled over many followers and afterwards went to Rome to negotiate an alliance, had actually penetrated into Media, the Romans being prevented by other wars at that time from interfering to prevent the inroad. The account given by those princes was that they had crossed a desert tract and afterwards a lake, which Romulus supposed to be the Maeotis, and after fifteen days journey surmounted a ridge of hills and descended into Media, which they began to ravage, but an immense host of Persian archers having come upon them, they were forced to fall back carrying with them only a small portion of the booty. Romulus therefore represented, that if Attila should determine to attack the Medes and Persians and Parthians, and render them tributary, he would find ready access to their territory, and had ample means to reduce them, against which no nation could make head successfully.

The party of Priscus having said that it was a consummation greatly to be desired, that Attila should be pleased to attack the Persians, and leave the empire at peace, were judiciously answered by Constantiolus that after the reduction of the Medes, Persians, and Parthians, Attila would be found still more formidable, and would no longer bear that the Roman empire should continue distinct from his own, but would treat them openly as his slaves; whereas at present he was contented with the payment of gold in consideration of the dignity conferred upon him; for, as Priscus witnesses, the degenerate Romans had bestowed upon their most dreaded antagonist the title of commander in chief over the Roman forces; but the Hun, not contented with the title by which, at the expense of national honor, they had hoped to sooth his vanity, demanded an ample stipend in the character of commander in chief; and even at that time in his angry moments he was wont to say, that his servants were the commanders of armies, and equal in honor with the emperors of Rome. "And yet (he adds) his power will erelong be greater, as the sword of Mars revealed by the God testifies, which being reputed sacred and worshipped by the Scythian kings as dedicated to the dispenser of battles, had disappeared in former times, but had been again found through the means of a heifer", which had been wounded by it, and left a track of blood that led to its discovery.

36. Banquet to which the ambassadors were invited by Attila.

Onegesius, having at length come forth, delayed answering the enquiries of Priscus, till he had conversed with some barbarians, after which he desired him to enquire from Maximin what man of consular dignity the Romans intended to send to treat with Attila, a question which must have been insolently intended, inasmuch as Maximin was of high rank and appointed for that special purpose.

Priscus having made this report and consulted with his principal, returned to answer the insult by a compliment to Onegesius, saying that the Romans would prefer that he should proceed to their court to adjust the points in controversy; but, if that could not be obtained, they would send whatever person would be most acceptable to Attila. Thereupon Onegesius desired Priscus to request the immediate presence of Maximin, whom he conducted straightway to the monarch.

Attila demanded that either Nomus or Anatolius or Senator should be sent to him, refusing to receive any other person in the character of ambassador. Maximin having represented to him, that by naming the persons with whom he chose to confer he could not fail to alarm the suspicions of Theodosius, he replied that unless they thought fit to do as he required, he would settle the controversy by the sword.

On the return of the ambassador and historian to the Roman tents, they were visited by the father of Orestes, who brought them an invitation from Attila to a banquet at the ninth hour of the day. At the appointed time the legates from the Eastern and Western empire, having proceeded together according to the invitation, stood at the threshold of the banqueting hall of Attila. After the fashion of the Hunnish court, the cupbearers, who were stationed near the door, placed a goblet in their hands, that they might drink a health to Attila before they took their places, to which they advanced after having tasted the cup. The seats were all placed against the wall on either side, but Attila sat on an elevated couch in the centre, another couch being placed behind him, from whence there was an ascent by means of steps to that on which he was seated.

The historian states that the seats on the right hand of Attila were considered the most honorable, and those on the left were secondary situations, which however were allotted to the Roman ambassadors, Bench, a noble Scythian, being placed above them. Onegesius sat upon a seat on the right beside the couch of Attila, and opposite to him on another seat were two of the monarch's sons. The eldest of the three, who were all children of Kreka, sat on the very couch of Attila, not beside him, but on the furthest edge, looking on the ground out of respect to his father. When the whole company were arranged in the several places destined for them, a cupbearer approaching Attila handed a goblet to him. Each guest had a particular cupbearer, whose duty it was to place himself in rank with the others, when the king's cup-bearer advanced.

Attila, having taken the goblet, saluted the person who occupied the first place, and he who was thus honored arose, nor was it lawful for him to sit down till having either emptied, or at least tasted, his own goblet, he had returned it to his cupbearer. In this manner Attila drank successively to the health of each of his convives, and, when he reseated himself, they returned the salutation, tasting the liquor after having addressed him. When this ceremony was ended, the cupbearers retired from the hall. Tables for three, four, or more guests, were placed behind that of Attila, where each person might help himself from the dish before him, but must not move from the place allotted to him. Then stepped forth the first attendant of Attila, bearing a dish filled with meat, and after him those who distributed bread and fish to the different tables. For the Romans and all the other guests a most sumptuous repast was furnished upon round silver plates, but the king himself ate nothing but flesh and that upon a wooden trencher, and showed like moderation in everything else, for the goblets of all his guests were of gold or of silver, but his own cup was also of wood. His dress was equally simple, being remarkable only for its perfect cleanness; and neither the formidable sword that hung beside him, nor the ligaments of his sandals, nor the bit of his horse was ornamented with gold and precious stones, like those of his followers. His personal appearance is recorded by Jornandes, extracting the description undoubtedly from Priscus, whom he cites immediately afterwards, but the original account is lost.

His stature was short, with a wide chest, a head of unusual magnitude, and small eyes which he had a habit of casting to the right and left with a haughty aspect; his beard was thin with an intermixture of grey hairs, his nose flat, and his complexion very dark, indicating his origin, as we are told by Jornandes, but whether he means simply that he had the peculiarities of the Hunnish race, or alludes to the diabolical extraction which he attributes to them, does not perfectly appear.

Having ate of the fish which was served on the first dishes, the whole company stood up, and no one might sit down again before he had quaffed to the bottom a cup full of wine, wishing health and prosperity to Attila. Having rendered him this honor, each person reseated himself, and proceeded to attack the second dish, which contained some other dainty; but after each dish had been finished, the same ceremony of standing up, and emptying a cup of wine to the monarch's health was repeated.

When the daylight began to fail, torches were lighted, and two barbarians, standing opposite to him, recited verses which they had composed, celebrating his victories, and the virtues which adorn a warrior. The guests appeared to listen to them with earnest attention, some delighted with the poetry, some excited by the recollections of the battles that were described, and others melting even into tears, their warlike spirit having been reduced by age to languish within a body no longer apt for military exertions.

When the songs were ended, a Scythian fool, uttering every sort of absurdity, made the whole court laugh. After him Zercon the Moor entered. He had come to the court, hoping by the good offices of Edécon to recover his wife, who, when he was a favorite with Bleda, had been given to him amongst the barbarians, but had been left by him in Scythia, when he was sent by Attila as a present to Aetius. He was ill-grown, short, hump-backed, with crooked legs, so excessively flat nosed, that there was scarcely any projection over his nostrils, and he lisped ridiculously. He had been formerly given to Aspar the son of Ardaburius, with whom he tarried some time in Lybia; but he was afterwards taken prisoner, when the Huns made an irruption into Thrace, and brought to the Hunnish kings. Attila hated to look on him, but Bleda took great delight in him, on account of the absurd things which he said, and his whimsical manner of walking and moving his body; and he kept him in his presence both at banquets and in warfare, and in his military expeditions he made him wear armour as a laughing-stock.

The ugly dwarf however contrived to make his escape with some other captives, but Bleda neglecting to pursue the others, ordered the most active search to be made after Zercon, and, when he was retaken and brought before him, he enquired why he preferred servitude under the Romans to his household; whereupon the Moor confessed his error, but attributed his flight entirely to the want of a wife. Bleda laughed exceedingly, and said that he should have one;

and in fact so absolute were the Hunnish kings, that he gave him in marriage a woman of noble birth, who had been an attendant on the queen, but on account of some unseasonable act was no longer permitted to approach her. He continued thus with Bleda until his death, when he was sent by Attila as a present to Aetius, who gave him back to Aspar. Having now returned to the court of Attila, he was disappointed in the hope of recovering his wife, because Attila was incensed at his having run away, when he had sent him as a present; but at this moment of festivity, by his look, his dress, and voice, and by the confusion of the words he used, blending in a ludicrous manner the language of the Goths and Huns with that of the Latins, he excited all the party, except Attila, to the most inextinguishable laughter; but Attila sat motionless, without the least change of countenance, and neither by word or sign showed any semblance of hilarity; excepting that he pinched the cheek of his youngest son by Kreka, named Ernas or Irnach, as he stood by him, and looked upon him with kindness. Priscus, having expressed his surprise, at his apparent preference for this child and neglect of the others, to a Scythian who sat by him and understood Latin, was told by him under promise of secrecy that it had been prophesied to Attila, that his race, which must otherwise be extinguished, would be upheld by this boy.

The carouse was prolonged far into the night, but the Romans, finding the potations inconveniently liberal, thought it advisable to withdraw; and on the following morning they visited Onegesius for the purpose of asking to be dismissed, and not kept wasting their time to no avail. They were informed by him that Attila desired their departure, and having left them for a short time he consulted with the select council concerning the wishes of Attila, and digested the letters which were to be sent to Theodosius with the assistance of certain scribes, and of Rusticius, who has been already mentioned, a native of Mysia who had been taken prisoner, and on account of his fluency in composition was retained in the epistolary department at the court of the Hun. The council being ended, the ambassadors applied to Onegesius for the liberation of the wife and children of Sylla, who had been captured in Ratiaria. He was not averse to set them free, but required an enormous ransom; whereupon they strove to move his compassion, by representing their former rank and condition, and their present misery. After having seen Attila again, he liberated the lady for 500 pieces of gold, and sent the children as a present to the emperor.

37. Rekan. Constantius.

In the meantime the ambassadors had received an invitation from Rekan the wife of Attila, to sup at the house of Adam the superintendant of her household and affairs;and having proceeded together with some of the principal Scythians, they were received with much courtesy, and fared sumptuously. Each of the guests paid them the singular compliment after the Hunnish fashion of standing up from the table and giving them a cup of wine, and, after they had drunk, embracing them and kissing them before he received back the cup. The supper was prolonged till it was time to retire to rest, and on the following day they were again invited to feast with Attila. The same forms were observed as on the former day, but instead of his elder son, Obarsius or Obars his uncle on the father's side sat on his couch.

During the repast the monarch spoke kindly to them, desiring them to request the emperor to send a wife, as he had promised, for Constantius the secretary who had been given to him by

Aetius. This Constantius, having previously accompanied the ambassadors whom Attila had sent to Theodosius, had promised that he would exert himself to make the peace durable, if the emperor would bestow a rich wife upon him, which was granted, and the daughter of Saturninus a rich and distinguished Greek, was promised to him. But Saturninus was afterwards assassinated by the empress Eudocia, and the emperor was prevented by Zeno, a man of consular dignity, from fulfilling his promise. This man had led a great force of Isaurians to the protection of Constantinople during the war, and, having then the command of all the forces in the East, he had withdrawn the damsel from the custody in which she had been placed, and had betrothed her to Rufus, one of his own dependants.

Constantius complained to the emperor of the insult and injustice done to him, and asked to have either the lady who had been thus abducted, or another bride of equal rank and opulence; on which account Attila enjoined to Maximin the care of the interests of his secretary, who undertook to give him a portion of the dowry, if he should succeed in obtaining one of the most wealthy Greek heiresses in marriage.

38. Berich accompanies the ambassadors on their return

Three days after, the ambassadors of Theodosius were dismissed with gifts, and with them Attila sent, on a mission to the emperor, Berich, who has been mentioned as having sat above them at the banquet. He was a member of the select council, and lord over many Scythian villages, and had been on some former occasion received by the Romans on an embassy.

During the journey, while they were tarrying in a certain village, a Scythian was taken, who had been sent as a spy by the Romans into the territory of Attila, who forthwith ordered him to be crucified. On the next day, as they were passing through another village, they saw two men who had formerly been taken prisoners in war, and were conducted with their hands tied behind them, having been guilty of murdering the masters to whom they had been allotted; and these were also crucified, their heads having been fixed to two beams furnished with hooks.

At the passage of the Danube, Berich, who had until then been exceedingly familiar and friendly, became very hostile and exasperated in consequence of some futile differences between the servants. He showed the first mark of resentment by redemanding a horse which he had given to Maximin; for Attila had ordered all the members of the select council to offer gifts to Maximin, and a horse had been sent by every one of them; Maximin however, wishing to get credit for moderation, had accepted only a few and sent back the remainder. Not content with requiring back his gift, Berich would no longer keep company with them on the road or eat with them; but having passed through Philippopolis and reached Adrianople, they came to an explanation with him, and a seeming reconciliation having taken place, they invited him to supper. On their arrival however at Constantinople it appeared that he still nourished the same resentment, alleging as a cause some offensive depreciation of Areobindus and Aspar by Maximin, detracting from their achievements in war, on account of the insignificance of the barbarians to whom they had been opposed, which he looked upon as an insult to himself and his countrymen.

39. Return of Bigilas.

On the way they had met Bigilas returning from Constantinople, and had informed him of the result of their mission. When Bigilas reached the quarter where Attila was then sojourning, he was seized by persons who had received previous directions to that effect, and the money which he was bringing for Edécon was taken from him. Being brought before Attila, he was asked, for what purpose he had brought so much gold; to which he replied, that he had brought it to supply himself and his companions with horses and other necessaries on the road, and with a view to ransom several captives, by whose relations he had been strenuously entreated; but Attila addressing him said, "Nevertheless, O malignant wild beast, you shall not by your sophistry escape judgment, nor will any pretext be sufficient to screen you from the infliction of punishment, for the money which thou hast in store is infinitely greater than necessary for thy expenses, or the purchase of horses and beasts of burden, or even for the ransom of captives, all which moreover I forbad you when thou earnest with Maximin". Having thus said, he ordered the son of Bigilas, who had been then for the first time brought to the Hunnish court, to be hewn down with the sword, unless he should forthwith declare unto whom and for what purpose he was bringing so much gold. But, when Bigilas beheld his son about to suffer death, he began to weep and lament, and cry out that justice demanded that he should be smitten with the sword, and not his son who was innocent of all offence; and without further delay he confessed all the things that had been devised between himself and Edécon, the eunuch Chrysaphius and the emperor, again imploring that he might be executed and not his son. Attila knowing from the previous report of Edécon that Bigilas had spoken the truth, directed him to be kept in chains, and threatened that he would not set him free, until his son should have been sent to Constantinople, and should have brought back other five hundred pieces of gold for their ransom. He therefore remained in custody, and his son was sent together with Orestes and Eslas to Constantinople.

40. His son sent to Constantinople.

The purse, in which the gold had been brought by Bigilas, was delivered to Edécon, and he was ordered by Attila to suspend it to his neck, and thus to enter the presence of the emperor, and having shown it to ask Chrysaphius whether he recognized it. Eslas was ordered to state that Theodosius was indeed the son of a noble father, and that Attila was also of noble birth, and had well sustained the nobility inherited from his father Mundiuc, but that Theodosius had fallen from his dignified station by submitting to pay tribute to him, and was become his slave; and that he therefore acted ill in devising secret snares like a wicked domestic against his superior, whom fortune had given him for his master. That Attila would not forgive the offence committed by him, unless the eunuch Chrysaphius were delivered up to undergo condign punishment. The storm, which was soon to burst on Chrysaphius, threatened him from more than one quarter; on the one side Attila demanded his life, on the other Zeno, incensed against the minister on account of the act of his master, who had confiscated to the public treasury the property of the daughter of Saturninus, whom Zeno had married to his dependant Theodosius had ordered the confiscation, being stung by the report of Maximin, who had stated that Attila had said that the emperor ought to fulfill his promise and give the lady to Constantius, for that no one amongst his subjects could have power to betroth her in contravention of his authority and engagements; that if the man who had dared to do so had not already suffered punishment for his temerity, the emperor was a slave to his own servants, and that he would willingly afford him assistance to emancipate him from their dominion.

41. Mission of Nomus and Anatolius.

The party of Chrysaphius, however, being prevalent at the court of Theodosius, it was determined to dispatch to Attila Anatolius master of the royal guard, who had proposed the terms of peace which had been concluded with the Huns, and Nomus having the title of master of the forces; both numbered amongst the patricians who had precedence over regular military rank. Nomus was sent with Anatolius, because he was very friendly to Chrysaphius, and Attila well disposed to receive him, and because he was also a man of great wealth, and was never sparing of money, when he had any object to accomplish. They were directed to use every endeavor to mollify Attila, and persuade him to adhere to the treaty which had been concluded; and to promise Constantius a wife in every respect as desirable as the lady of whom he had been disappointed; assuring him that the daughter of Saturninus had been averse to the alliance proposed, and was lawfully wedded to another; and that the Roman law did not authorize the betrothment of a woman to any man without her own consent.

Chrysaphius sent a present of gold to pacify the offended monarch. The mission of Theodosius having crossed the Danube proceeded through the territory of the Huns as far as the Drencon or Drecon; for Attila, through respect for Anatolius and Nomus whom he esteemed, advanced towards them and met them on the banks of that river, to save them a further journey. At first he spoke to them in the most over-bearing tone, but at length their gifts and conciliatory language prevailed over his irritated temper, and he consented to keep the peace, and gave up to the Romans all the land he claimed to the south of the Danube, and waived his demands for the restoration of fugitives, on condition that the Romans should pledge themselves to receive none in future. He also set free Bigilas, having received the 500 pounds of gold which his son had brought with the embassy; and he further, to show his kindness towards Nomus and Anatolius, liberated several captives without any ransom; and he dismissed the ambassadors with presents of horses and skins of wild beasts, such as were usually worn for ornament by the Scythian kings.

Constantius was directed to proceed with them on their return to Constantinople, that he might obtain without further delay, the rich heiress promised to him by the emperor; nor was the secretary unsuccessful in this expedition, but consummated his nuptials with the widow of Armatius, the son of Plinthas, who had been a Roman general and consul. The lady was both rich and noble, and espoused Constantius at the request of the emperor. It is impossible to contemplate these transactions, of which Priscus, who was engaged in them, has left such minute particulars, without blushing at the perfidious villainy of the Chris-tian court, and admiring the noble magnanimity and moderation of the pagan on this occasion; but it was perhaps the policy of Attila to represent his own life to be so protected by the great destinies for which he pretended to have been foredoomed, that such attempts against it were very unimportant and certain of ending in discomfiture; and it might be more for his interest to treat them with scorn, than to attract attention to them by a public execution.

In the whole career of his life he was disposed to clemency when it did not militate against the success of his undertakings, but inexorable and remorseless where it was his interest to disarm opposition by the terror of his exterminating vengeance. The indiscriminate slaughter of the inhabitants of a town captured after an obstinate defence, might deter another from resisting, but he must have been aware that those, who had entered into a direct conspiracy against his life, must have done so with the certain expectation of crucifixion if they should foil; and that the punishment, if inflicted, would add nothing to the motives which necessarily existed to deter men from engaging in so desperate an undertaking; and that treating it lightly, as a vain and impracticable scheme which it was not worth his while to punish, might be the best mode of deterring the superstitious from attempting it. It is most remarkable that his personal respect and deference for Nomus and Anatolius should have won from him in the plenitude of his strength and at the very moment when he must have been most irritated by the treacherous and disgusting designs of Theodosius, concessions which would in vain have been sought for by an appeal to arms.

42. Mission of Apollonius.

The empire, however, though relieved from the immediate fear of Attila, was threatened with internal dissensions, and Zeno became a formidable rival to his master. The sword of Attila, though sheathed, was ever ready for fresh contests, and he appears to have been in the following year (AD 450) excited to new threats of invasion, in consequence of the non-payment of the stipulated tribute by the emperor.

Apollonius, brother to Rufus then defunct, to whom Zeno had given the daughter of Saturninus, friendly to Zeno upon that account, and bearing the rank of general, was despatched to pacify Attila; but, having crossed the Danube, he was denied access to him: for Attila was enraged at the retention of the tribute, which he said had been arranged and agreed upon by men better and more worthy to reign than Theodosius, and he therefore rejected the ambassador, to show his contempt for the emperor; but, although he refused to admit his messenger, or to enter into any negotiation, he nevertheless ordered the gifts of Theodosius to be sent to him, and threatened Apollonius with death if he should deny them. The ambassador however showed a spirit worthy of the ancient fortunes of Rome, and replied, that it did not become the Scythians to ask for what they must take either as gifts, or by plunder; signifying that he was ready to give them if his embassy was received, but that the Huns must take them as booty if they thought fit to assassinate him. Attila, however, though he frequently indulged in such threats, appears in fact to have always respected the immunity conferred on ambassadors by the common consent of nations; and the high-minded Roman was dismissed without having been admitted into his presence.

43. Death of Theodosius. Marcian. Honoria.

Theodosius did not live to feel the effects of the anger of Attila, from whom it is probable that he withheld the promised tribute in consequence of the exhausted state of his finances, rather than a determination to brave his animosity. A fall from his horse terminated the life of this inglorious and degraded emperor. His sister Pulcheria, was proclaimed empress without opposition, although there had been no previous instance of a female succeeding to the throne; and the first act of her reign was the execution of Chrysaphius without a legal trial, before the gates of Constantinople. Fearful however of swaying the scepter of the East without the support of a stronger arm at so critical a period, she immediately espoused the senator Marcian, a Thracian about sixty years of age, who had served with credit under Aspar and Ardaburius; but, though she invested him by this political union with the imperial purple, she compelled him in wedlock to respect the religious vow which she had made of perpetual virginity.

As soon as Attila heard of the accession of Marcian to the throne, he sent to demand the stipulated tribute, but Marcian adopted a higher tone than his predecessor, and replied that he did not hold himself bound by the humiliating concessions of Theodosius; that he would send presents to him, if he kept the peace, but, if he threatened war, he would oppose to him arms and men by no means inferior to his own forces.

At this period the intrigue of Honoria with Attila had been discovered, and had brought down upon her the indignation and vengeance of either empire. The extract, which is extant from the history of Priscus, relating to this subject, refers to a previous relation of the circumstances which had taken place, but, that being lost, their particulars can only be imperfectly collected or surmised from subsequent allusions. At the voluptuous court of Ravenna, that princess celebrated for her beauty and her incontinence, while she continued still under the guardianship of Placidia her mother and her brother Valentinian, in the very spring of her youth, sixteen years before this period, had been found pregnant by her chamberlain Eugenius, and had been disgracefully sent from thence to Constantinople, to be immured in the secluded chambers of Pulcheria the sister of Theodosius, who had made a vow of singleness, and dwelt in a sworn society of holy virgins. Weary of the monotonous and hopeless mode of life in which her youth was thus passing away, under the tutelage of her harsh and sanctified relation, she had probably at a much earlier period, made a tender to Attila of her hand and pretensions to the throne of Rome, and that offer, to which on his first accession to the throne, he had paid little attention, had been renewed a little before this period, when his matured designs against the empire rendered such an alliance important, as a ground whereon to rest his claims.

The message was carried to Attila by an eunuch despatched by the princess secretly from Constantinople with a letter and a ring, which he was instructed to deliver, but the exact date of the occurrence is not recorded. At the moment of the accession of Marcian to the throne, the correspondence of Honoria with the Hun was by some accident brought to light. The unfortunate and guilty princess was regarded with abhorrence by the Christians, and previously to her being sent back to Italy and placed in strict confinement at Ravenna, she was compelled to give her hand in marriage to some person who was selected for that purpose, in order to render her union with Attila unlawful and impracticable. The records are lost which would have informed us who and what the bridegroom was, but it is pretty evident that the ceremony only was performed, and that the marriage was not consummated; and as it was certainly not intended that she should ever avail herself of the privileges of a married woman, the husband selected for her was probably an obscure and perhaps a blind old man, for the extinction of the eyes was the usual mode of disqualifying a man to wear the imperial purple of Constantinople.

In the passage of Priscus which is preserved, and which evidently refers to a detailed account of the transactions, he says that when the things which had been done concerning her were reported to Attila, he immediately sent ambassadors to Valentinian emperor of the West, to assert that Honoria had been guilty of no unbecoming conduct, inasmuch as he had entered into an engagement to marry her, and that he would take up arms in her cause, unless she were admitted to hold the scepter of the empire. The Romans answered that it was not possible for him to espouse Honoria, who had been given to another man, and that she had no right to the throne, for the Roman dynasty consisted of a succession of males, and not of females: an answer which singularly contrasts with the contemporaneous and undisputed elevation of Pulcheria to the sister throne of Byzantium, occasioned perhaps by some intrigues for the downfall of Chrysaphius.

The rejection of the demands of Attila by Marcian had been softened by presents, and probably the refusal of Honoria's hand was accompanied by like appeasement. According to the Alexandrine or Paschal chronicle, and to John of Antioch, surnamed Malellas, Attila sent to either emperor a Gothic messenger, saying, "My lord and yours commands you through me to make ready your palace for his reception". Malellas mentions Theodosius, who was dead at this time; but the account is probably referable to the simultaneous summons which he sent to Constantinople and Rome immediately after the death of that emperor.

44. Views of Attila on Gaul—Court in Thuringia.

The views of Attila extended to the subjugation of the Medes and Persians, the Eastern and Western empires, and the Gothic and Franc kingdoms in France and Spain, which would have left him without a rival between the boundaries of China, or at least of the Tartars, and the Atlantic ocean : but he was awhile doubtful against which of those powers he should first turn his arms. Genseric the formidable king of the Vandals, who had wrested from Rome her African possessions, excited him to attack Theodoric king of the Visigoths, whose capital was Tolosa, the modern Toulouse. The daughter of Theodoric had been married to Hunneric the son of the Vandal monarch, who was so savage in his disposition, and inhuman even towards his own offspring, that on a bare suspicion that she had mixed poison for him, he cut off her nostrils and sent her back mutilated to her father. Fearing therefore the vengeance of Theodoric, he exerted himself by negotiation and ample presents to draw upon his antagonist the overwhelming armies of the Hun. The subsidy offered by Genseric probably determined

Attila to commence his operations by the subjugation of Gaul, where he would have to attack the Francs of Meroveus, the Alans under Sangiban, the Gallic empire of Theodoric extending from his capital Tolosa into Spain, and the Roman province which was defended by the flower of the Roman army under the celebrated Aetius. The pretext for this invasion was the restitution of Alberon, the son and rightful heir of Clodion lately deceased, to the throne of his father in the north of France, from whence he had been expelled by the arts of the bastard Meroveus. Previous to his undertaking this memorable expedition, Attila held a plenar court or comitia in Thuringia at Erfurt, (for Eisenach, which has been named as the place where they were held, is perhaps a town of later origin) probably for the especial purpose of hearing the plaint of Basina the widow of Clodion, who had fled with her sons to the court of her brother Basinus in Thuringia.

45. Eudoxius. Bagauds. Meroveus. Alberon.

Eudoxius, a physician, had been drawn into a faction of rebels in Gaul, who, being pushed to extremities by the extortions of the nobles and clergy, had first revolted in the reign of Diocletian under the denomination of Bagauds, and had since made head under the guidance of Tibato against the Roman authority. They were everywhere defeated and severely handled, and Eudoxius was the only man of importance amongst the movers of that sedition who escaped, and he took refuge at the Hunnish court. He is described as a bad, but able, man; and from him it is supposed that Attila received much information concerning the actual state of Gaul, and encouragement to attempt its invasion. It is observable, that the organization of the faction called Bagauds seems to have been the only popular attempt to vindicate civil rights under the domination of the Western emperors.

Meroveus, against whom the arms of Attila were now directed, was the illegitimate son of Clodion, and his master of the horse. The dynasty of the Marcomirians ended with Clodion the son of Pharamond and grandson of Marcomir; and Meroveus, a traitor, an usurper, and alien to the blood royal, being illegitimate, founded a new dynasty. Fredegarius, writing in 641, says that the mother of Meroveus was bathing on the coast and was attacked by a sea-monster, who became the father of Meroveus. This fable has evident relation to his illegitimacy. The writer who there cites Fredegarius from Gregory of Tours considers the Marobudos or Maroboduus who lived in the time of Augustus and Tiberius to have been an earlier Meroveus, the former name being the Augustan, the latter the recent Gallo-Latin version of the Teutonic name Maerwu or Merwu. He also shows that the Merovingian kings called themselves by that title, (which makes it appear that they affected to be a new dynasty, and not inheritors from Clodion) by authorities dating AD 641 as above, AD 645 and 720, the last being thirty years before the restoration of the rightful heirs by the elevation of Pepin.

Mezeray states that Clodion left three sons (the eldest having died) Alberon, Regnault, and Rangcaire, who were too young to reign, and therefore the states elected Meroveus his bastard son. He boasts of his exploits in the Catalaunian victory, of which he attributes the principal honor to him, but entirely suppresses the cause of that war, which was to re-establish the rightful king whom he had expelled: and he adds incorrectly that, when firmly fixed in Gaul, he went to succor the sons of Clodion and establish them in Hainault, Brabant, and Namur; saying that on his return from that expedition he died in the tenth year of his reign in 458.

The historian Priscus, who was at the court of Attila on an embassy in 448, when Clodion was alive or on the point of death, never saw Alberon the rightful heir, who had not at that time had recourse to the Huns. At some antecedent period not ascertained, he had however seen Meroveus on an embassy at Rome, a beardless youth with long yellow hair falling over his shoulders, and he says that Aetius, having adopted him as his son and loaded him with gifts, despatched him to the emperor to acquire his friendship and enjoy his society in martial exercises. There is some obscurity however in the passage, for the word presbenúmenos, acting the part of a legate, must apply to a mission from the Francs, and could not refer to his visit at the court of Valentinian under the recommendation of the Roman general Aetius.

It seems that Priscus meant that Meroveus was at Rome as an ambassador when he saw him, and was at some subsequent period sent by Aetius to carouse with Valentinian, probably at Ravenna.

Looking to the subtle character and constant double dealing of Aetius, it can scarcely be doubted, that when he adopted Meroveus and sent him to Valentinian, he had intended to sow future dissensions in the family of Clodion, and to make use of Meroveus for the furtherance of his own schemes, whether against the inheritance of the Franc king or against the throne of Valentinian, or, as is most probable, against both: and, in directing him to be pre-sented to the emperor as the son of Clodion, with a view to the acquisition of his society and friendship, it is not likely that either Aetius or Meroveus should have put forward his illegitimacy; nor was it probable that Priscus, a Greek sophist of Constantinople, accidentally seeing this beardless young Franc at Rome, should have been informed at the time of his spurious birth. When Meroveus seized the throne and expelled Alberon who fled to the Huns, it was a matter of notoriety to all Europe that Alberon was the rightful heir and eldest son of Clodion, and if Priscus was not aware of the illegitimacy of Meroveus, he must have concluded that he was younger than him to whom the inheritance appertained. His silence as to the name of the banished king is proof that he had not very ample information concerning the transaction, and perhaps only knew the little which he states; and, living at Constantinople far from the scene of action, he may have fallen very naturally into an error on the point of seniority. If Meroveus had succeeded to the throne of his lawful father, though to the prejudice of an elder brother, his accession would not have been that of a new dynasty, and, instead of being called Merovingian kings, he and his descendants would from the first have been named after Pharamond the sire or Marcomir the grandsire of Clodion.

The brief expression therefore of Priscus, that the elder son of Clodion sought the assistance of the Huns, the younger that of Aetius, is insufficient to outweigh the far greater probability of the fact as related by other writers, that Meroveus was in fact the oldest, though not the legitimate, son of Clodion. The lineal genealogy runs thus:— 1. Marcomir.—2. Pharamond.—3. Clodion who died 448.—4. Alberon, d.491.—5. Wambert, d. 529—6. Ambert, d. 570. (collateral Wambert 2.)—7. Arnold, d. 601.—8. St. Arnulf, d. 641.—9. Ansegisus, d. 685.—10. Pepin, d. 714.—11. Charles Martell, d. 741.—12. Pepin, d. 768.—13. Charlemagne, and so on, till the occupation of the throne by Hugh Capet in 987, when the Marcomirian line became extinct.

John Bertels abbot of Epternach collected all the traditions and chronicles he could find in the convents of Luxemberg and Ardennes. He states that Clodion Capillatus married Basina daughter of Widelph duke of the Thuringians, probably sister to Basinus who was duke when Attila was in Thuringia. She bore him four sons, Phrison, Alberon or Auberon, Reginald, and Rauchas. Phrison died very young of an arrow-shot, and the grief of that loss hastened the death of his father. Clodion by his will appointed his bastard son Meroveus, who was his master of the horse, to be regent and guardian of his sons.

For some years he acted with fidelity, but when the Roman arms were pressing on the Francs, he tendered his resignation, declining the responsibility of administering the affairs of another person in such a crisis, and knowing that his authority and skill were necessary at the moment. The result was conformable to his expectations. The Francs proclaimed him king, and he took the crown, whereupon queen Basina sent her three sons for safety to Thuringia. Some years afterwards Alberon took counsel how he should recover his rights and destroy Meroveus and his progeny; Meroveus at the same time meditating the like against him and his kindred.

With these views Alberon married Argotta daughter of Theodemir king of the Goths, formed a strict alliance with the Goths, Vandals, Bohems, and Ostrogoths, and by their aid recovered possession of Arduenna, Lower Alsatia, Brabantia, Cameracum, and Turnacum, and obtained the title of Rex Cameracensis. His chief residence however was in the Nemus Carbonarium, a part of the forest of Ardennes, where he sacrificed to idols and fortified Mons Hannoniae (Mons in Hainault), as an asylum against the malice of Meroveus. Argotta bore him Wambert, who married a daughter of the emperor Zeno.

A lieutenant under Clovis conquered Brabant and Flanders about the year 492, and took king Alberon and his two brothers prisoners, whom the French king barbarously slew with his own hand, as soon as they were brought into his presence. He afterwards affected remorse, and endeavored to allure Wambert into his power, in order to cut off the last remnant of Clodion's legitimate heirs. Wambert was however too wary, and placed his sons Wambert and Anselbert (or Ambert), under the safeguard of Theodoric king of Italy and the emperor Zeno who made them senators of the Eastern empire.

About AD 520 Wambert recovered Ardennes and Hainault, to which possessions the senator Wambert the second succeeded on his death in 528, by favor of Childebert king of Paris, who also gave Anselbert the marquisate of Moselle and Scheld, of which the seat of government was on the latter river. The senator Wambert, who espoused St. Clotilda daughter of Almeric king of Italy, was succeeded by a third Wambert his son.

Such is the statement of Bertels. The only inaccuracy, which appears on the face of it, is that the events, which took place between the death of Clodion in 448, and the flight of Alberon to the Huns previous to Attila's invasion of Gaul in 451, a space of only three years, appear to be extended over a longer, though indefinite, period. With this limitation, that Meroveus could not have continued faithful above two years, and that Alberon immediately sought assistance to recover his rights, there is no reason to doubt that the account of Bertels is substantially correct. He was unacquainted with the writings of Priscus, and appears to have known nothing about Attila and his Huns; yet, except what relates to the inferior age of Meroveus, he affords collateral evidence from quite different sources, which is confirmed by the account of the Greek sophist; for it is evident that the Goths, with whom Bertels states Alberon to have made alliance, were the great confederacy of nations headed by Attila and brought by him on the occasion of the disputed succession of Clodion into the celebrated field of Chalons.

The Thuringian writers of the middle ages make mention of the movements of Attila, and state that he was in Thuringia and at Eisenach. The Danish writer, professor Suhm, referring to the Thuringian authors, states his disbelief of the existence of Eisenach in the days of Attila, and thinks that Erfurt, anciently called Bicurgium, was the place intended. Sidonius Apollinaris mentions Toringus (the Thuringian) amongst the people who invaded Belgium under the command of Attila. German histories unknown to Bertelius and only seen in MS. by Lazius, affirm that Attila held a diet of his kings and dukes in Thuringia before he set out to invade Gaul. Putting these concurrent accounts together, it seems that Attila held a diet in Thuringia, where he heard the plaint of queen Basina and her sons, and proceeded to act thereupon. Henning in his Universal Genealogy gives the following statement: Clodio crinitus had, by ..., Meroveus, who married Verica daughter of Guntraum king of Sweden, and died AD 458, and by Basina daughter of Widelph king of Thuringia Albero or Alberic from whom the Carolingians are descended, Rauches or Roches lord of Cambray, and Reginald king of the Eburi who married Wamberga daughter of Alaric the first king of the Visigoths in Spain. Albero warred under Attila, hoping to recover the scepter of his father, of which his brother Meroveus had taken forcible possession. Being defeated he retreated to his own people, (meaning his Belgic or Cameracan subjects) being careful not to fall into the hands of Meroveus, and died about 491.

46. Merovingians. Kingdom of Cameracum

Brother James of Guise relates that Clodion king of the Francs had by his wife, daughter of the king of Austrien (Austracia) and Toringien, four sons. He made a certain Meroveus his master of the horse. Soon after, besieging Soissons, he lost his eldest son, and, being much afflicted, died also. Previously he assembled his nobles, and assigned to his wife and each of his three remaining sons their portions, and gave them into the keeping of Meroveus. Meroveus enlarged the kingdom by conquest; afterwards, some enemies invading it, he said to the people, "I am not your king, and I will no longer be the guardian, for I have already incurred more cost than I can pay; therefore provide for the country as you will". Consequently the Francs raised him to the throne. He straightway summoned all the soldiers that were on furlough, and drove out the enemy. The widow of Clodion, with two of her sons, fled to Thuringia and Austracia. When big enough, they redemanded the kingdom, and had some combats with Meroveus. By the assistance of the Huns, Goths, Ostrogoths, Armoricans, Saxons, and many others, they won back from Meroveus the lands their father had assigned them, beginning from Austracia to the Alsatic mountains, and from the south of Burgundy to the Rhine, and westward to Rheims, Laon, Cambray, and Tournay, and on the north to the ocean, which kingdom was molested by Meroveus and many others. From Clodion's three sons, Aubron, Regnauld, and Rauchaure, the rulers of Hainault, Loraine, Brabant, and Namur, took their origin. Clodion was buried at Cambray in 448 according to the rites of the "Sarrazins". He adds that many opinions existed touching Meroveus.

According to Sigebert he was the son of Clodion; Andreas Marcianensis styled him his kinsman (son afin, meaning affinis); l'histoire des Francois states that he was not his son, but nevertheless descended from the Trojans, and that he was a useful king, from whom were derived the Francs called Merovingians, who held the kingdom against the heirs of Clodion. Almericus states that after Bleda's death, the widow of Clodion made alliance with the Huns and Ostrogoths, gave them a part of her land, and waged war against Meroveus. Brother James continues to say that in 453 (he should have said 451) Attila, accompanied by Walamir king of the Ostrogoths, and Arderic king of the Gepidae, and many of their dependants from the quarter of the wind aquilon, left Pannonia and invaded Gaul. Alberic or Aubron, second son of Clodion, was a man of such subtlety, knowledge, activity, and prowess, that he often worsted the Merovingians, who usurped and held his country.

He commonly sojourned in the woods, and sacrificed to Gods and Goddesses, and re-established the pagan worship in his territories, for he thought the Gods in whom he trusted would give him back his kingdom; because Mars and Jove had once appeared to him, and declared that to himself, or to his lineage, all the dominions of his father should be restored. Thereupon he began assiduously to rebuild the decayed cities and castles, Strasburg which was dismantled of walls, Thulle, Espinal, Mereasse, and the leaden baths at Espinal; in the forest of Dogieuse a castle and temples; near the Alsatic mountains and forests the same; in the centre of his kingdom in Ardenne, the altar, temple, and castle of Namur; the temple of Mercury, now chateau Sanson, and other impregnable forts; in the forêt Carboniere many, such as Chateaulieu, where on the mount he built a square tower, and called it from himself Aubron.

On the same mount, near the town, he dug a well which is still there. He built a temple of Minerva on a hill, now mount St. Audebert, but then mount Auberon, but which the Christians now call La Houppe Auberon; in the forest of Dicongue a temple of the idol, and called it by his own name. By the aid of the Saxons he beat the Merovingians in the forêt Carboniere near Chateaulieu, now called Monts en Haynau, and he named the spot Merowinge, and the inhabitants now call it Meuwin. He beat them again at a place called Mirewault, and the Merovingians said the Gods of the forest gave him victory, and thereupon remained a long time at peace with him. They styled him enchanteur of feu. He had several children; the eldest Waubert, who was king of the Austracians, and inherited all his father's lands and defended them valiantly. Aubron died old, and was buried with Sarrazin rites in the mount called La Houppe Auberon, upon which great trees are now planted.

Clovis invaded the lands of the king of Cambray called Rauchaire, brother of Auberon, and at last he and his brothers Richier and Regnault, were betrayed into his power, and slain by his own hand; and he persecuted their connections. Here is an evident blunder, in the calling Rauchaire instead of Auberon, king of Cambray, and then to make up the number, repeating the name Rauchaire with a difference of orthography, as Richier, and thus making five sons of

Basina, instead of four, the eldest having been killed at the siege of Soissons in the life-time of Clodion.

The history thus given contains ample confirmation to the relation of Bertels, with a similar protraction of the period between the death of Clodion, and the attempt of Alberon to recover his throne, which is in some degree accounted for by placing in 453 the Hunnish invasion, which actually took place in 451. That Meroveus did not pretend to be the legitimate son of Clodion, is evident from the expression of Gregory Tours, who flourished in the next century, and might even hate conversed with persons who had seen Meroveus, and merely says that he was "as some assert, of the stock of Clodion".

No reliance can be placed on the relation of any French writer of later times, for, without citing any satisfactory authorities, they all avoid the true point, and falsify the history, so strangely does nationality and a desire to make out the dynasty of their kings to have been legitimate appear to have warped and prejudiced their understandings; in the same manner that we find the Danish historians when they meet with the name of Attila king of the Huns, in their most ancient legends of events, which they themselves refer to the exact period of his Gallic invasion, shutting their eyes against the true history, and saying that this Attila was a petty king over some Huns in Groningen, because they will not acknowledge that which Priscus, who was personally acquainted with Attila, asserts, that his dominion extended to the Baltic or islands of the ocean, and consequently that he was, as appears also from the title he assumed, king of the Danes.

That Meroveus was received at Rome as the son of Clodion, is clear by the testimony of Priscus; that he was illegitimate and older than the rightful heir, is established by the local chronicles and the greater probability of the fact. Whether Alberon was put to death as well as his brothers by Clovis, or fell in the previous battle, and was buried in the Houppe d' Aubron, appears to be a matter of some doubt, which perhaps might be solved at this day, by opening the supposed place of his interment; but it is not improbable that his name affixed to that mount, as a monumental cenotaph, may have given birth to the notion that he was buried there, and occasioned the omission of his name in some of the accounts of the atrocious act of Clovis, especially as there is no other tradition of the manner of his death, though so many particulars of his life are recorded.

47. Valentinian excites Theodoric against Attila.

When Attila had determined to march his army into Gaul, he exerted himself to sow disunion between the Visigoths and Romans. He sent ambassadors to Valentinian to assure him in a letter full of blandishment that he had no hostile intentions against the Roman power in that country, but was marching against Theodoric, and requested that the Romans would not take part against him. To Theodoric he wrote at the same time, exhorting him to detach himself from his alliance with the Romans, and to remember the wars which they had lately stirred up against him. Thereupon the emperor wrote to Theodoric urging him to act in union with him against the common enemy, "who wished to reduce the whole world to slavery; who sought no pretext for invasion, but held whatever his arm could execute to be just and right; who grasped at everything within his compass, and satiated his licentiousness with excess of pride". He represented to the Visigoth that he ruled over a limb of the Roman empire, and exhorted him for his own security to unite with the Romans in defending their common interests.

Theodoric replied, "Ye have your wish; ye have made Attila and me enemies. We will encounter him, whithersoever he shall call us, and, although he may be inflated by diverse victories over proud nations, haughty as he is, the Goths will know how to contend with him. I call no warfare grievous, except that which its cause renders weak, for he, on whom majesty has smiled, has no reverse to fear".

The chiefs of the Gothic court applauded this spirited answer, of which however the last words do not convey any very definite meaning. The people shouted and followed him, and the Visigoths were animated by an ardent desire to measure their strength with the conqueror of so many nations.

48. Attila advances against Gaul.

In the spring of 451 Attila put his immense army in motion to effect the invasion of Gaul. Many of the nations that marched under him are enumerated by Sidonius; the Neuri, who are stated by Ammianus Marcellinus to have dwelt amongst the Alans in their former situations; the Hoedi, whom Valesius asserts to have been a tribe of Huns; the Gepides, Ostrogoths, Alans, Bastarnae, Turcilingi, Scirri, Heruli, Rugi, Bellonoti, Sarmatae, Geloni, Scevi, Burgundiones, Quadi, Marcomanni, Savienses or Suavi, Toringi, (Thuringians) the Franks who bordered on the river Vierus, and the Bructeri, who were considered to be allied to the Francs in blood. Aventhius mentions also the Boii, Suevi, and Alemanni under king Gibuld. In Henning's Genealogies it is said that a hundred nations marched under Attila. This immense army pursued its course south of the Danube, and passed through Noricum and the northern part of Rhaetia, that is to say the southern parts of Bavaria and Swabia. His northern vassals the Rugians, Quadi, Marcomanni, Thuringians, and other tribes followed, it seems, a more northerly course, having directions to form a junction with him on the Rhine.

Near the lake of Constance he was probably opposed by and routed a portion of the Burgundians, who were in the interest of Aetius, and attempted to prevent him from passing the Rhine. Aventinus says that he slew on that occasion their kings Gundaric and Sigismund, which does not appear to be correct, at least with respect to Gundaric.

The forests of Germany, almost indiscriminately called Hercynian, furnished him with timber to construct vessels or rafts, on which the immense multitude, which constituted his army, was transported across the Rhine. Strasburg probably first felt the effects of his fury, and was leveled to the ground. At a later period, a figure of Attila is said to have been placed over the gate of that town. Some writers have asserted, that Metz (Divodurum Mediomatricorum) was the first place that he destroyed; thither he certainly proceeded and burnt the town, butchering its inhabitants, and the very priests at the altars. His march was directed towards the Belgian territory, and, having sacked Treves on his route, he overwhelmed the north of France, destroying whatever resisted him. Whether Tongres and Maastricht were destroyed before or after the battle of Chalons, is not certain. No effectual resistance could be offered to him by the Francs under Meroveus, and Alberon was speedily reinstated in the greater part of the kingdom of Clodion.

49. Aetius prepares to oppose him. Note concerning Danes.

At this time Aetius, having expected that Theodoric would have made head against Attila, and probably wishing that they might weaken each other by the collision, his own forces remaining untouched, while Attila was overrunning all Belgium, had scarcely crossed the Alps, leading with him a small and very inefficient force. But intelligence was brought to him of the unexampled successes of Attila, and that the Visigoths, appearing to despise the Huns, whom they had formerly beaten when subsidized by Litorius, were awaiting in their own territory the attack of the invader, if he should think fit to bear down upon them.

The active mind of Aetius was equal to the arduous position in which he stood. He immediately dispatched Avitus to urge Theodoric to draw out his force without delay and form a junction with him. His exertions were great and rapid to collect a force sufficient to make head against the conqueror, who was already preparing to fall upon the south of France. Theodoric, accompanied by his two eldest sons Torismond and Theodoric, took the field, having ordered his four younger sons to remain at Tolosa, to which he himself was not destined to return. The wonderful genius and activity of Aetius, when it suited his views to bestir himself, was never more conspicuous than on this occasion, when he speedily brought together a force equal to that of the Hun. In the allied army the Visigoths of Theodoric, the Alans of king Sangiban, the Francs of Meroveus, Sarmatians, Armoricans, Burgundians, Saxons, Litiarii, Riparioli, and several other German and Celtic nations were united with the Romans. Although the affairs of Attila are conspicuous in the Northern legends, it is observable that, in the vast concourse of tribes pouring into France from every quarter of Europe, no mention is made by any writer of Danes, for this simple reason that there was in truth no such nation at that period, other than the Dacians from the Danube, notwithstanding the assertions of Danish historians.

50. Siege of Orleans.

The attack of Paris did not fall within the line of Attila's operations, and the Christians subsequently attributed the salvation of that city to the merits of St. Genevieve; but Paris was not then a great metropolis. The late king Clodion had had his principal seat at Dispargum, supposed by some to have been Louvain, but probably Duysberg on the right bank of the Rhine. It was apparently one of the effects of Attila's invasion, by detaching Cambray,

Hainault, and the rest of the Belgic provinces from the kingdom of Meroveus, to make Paris become the seat of his government. Tolosa, the flourishing capital of Theodoric the Visigoth, was an object of superior importance to Attila. He had already, in pursuance of his intentions, reduced again under the authority of Alberon the greater part of the Belgic portion of the kingdom of the Francs; and his promises to make a powerful diversion in favor of Genseric king of the Vandals in Africa, and his own ambitious views, pointed to the south of France. His main force was therefore directed against Orleans; from whence, if he had been successful, he would have undoubtedly continued f his victorious course towards the Gothic metropolis, or Arelas the principal city of the Roman province.

We know not to whom the military defence of Orleans was entrusted. Sangiban, king of the Alans, who occupied the neighborhood of the Loire, was at that time in Orleans, but he does not appear to have had the command of the garrison. In the history of these times, whether relating to the Gallic war, or the invasion of Italy, we hear more of the bishop of the place, who seems generally to have taken upon himself the chief conduct of affairs, than of any military prefect; partly, perhaps, because the details which have reached us have been chiefly transmitted through ecclesiastics. To the bishop, therefore, has been generally attributed both the vigour that defended, and the treason that surrendered to the pagan, the fortresses of the Roman empire; the traitors and the martyrs seem to have found a place equally in the calendar of saints. Anianus, since called St. Aignan, held the see of Orleans, when the immense force of Attila proceeded to invest it. He made every disposition for a stout defence, encouraged the people and the garrison to put their confidence in God, without relaxing their efforts, and despatched a trusty messenger to Aetius, urging him to advance immediately to his relief.

The operations of the Hun were perhaps impeded for a few days by unseasonable weather, but his engines battered the town with irresistible force, and it seemed as if nothing but the direct interposition of Providence could save the town and its inhabitants from the terrible chastisement, which Attila never failed to inflict upon those who presumed to defend themselves. Bishop Anian prayed, and prayed, and prayed; but the walls were shaken by the force of the battering rams, the garrison were driven from the battlements by the Hunnish archery, and the battlements themselves crumbled under the repeated shocks of the blocks of stone that were hurled by the machines of the besiegers. He sent his attendant to look out and report whether he saw anything in the distance. The answer was, no. Again he sent him, and nothing was distinguishable.

A third time, and he reported, like the messenger of Elijah, that a little cloud was rising on the plain. The bishop shouted to the people, that it was the aid of God, and throughout the whole town there was a cry of the aid of God, mingled with the shrieks of women; for at that very instant the Huns were scaling the breach and actually in the town, and in a few moments the city would have been a blazing and bloody example of barbarian vengeance. But Attila had seen the little cloud that was advancing in the distance, and recognized the dust that was raised by the rapid advance of the Gothic cavalry, which formed the van of the army of Aetius. Instantly he saw the danger of exposing his troops to the attack of a powerful enemy under that cosummate general, amidst the disorganization which must accompany the sack of a populous city, which was on the point of being delivered up to plunder; and at the very instant when

Orleans was taken, and the work of violation and massacre was on the point of commencing, the successful assailants were astonished by the signal for a retreat.

The deliverance was attributed by the Christians to the direct interposition of Providence, obtained by the faith and supplications of their priest.

51. Retreat of Attila to the Catalaunian plain.

Attila did not think it expedient to await the attack of Aetius before the walls of a hostile town, and, having learned the strength of the allied army, he retreated to the great plains of Champagne which took their name from Catalannum, the modern Châlons upon Marne, and by that movement he probably fell back upon his own resources and concentrated his forces, for it is not likely that the whole of his enormous army should have been in the lines before Orleans. He knew that he had to contend with a general of great skill, a king of approved valor, and an army equal to his own in numbers and warlike habits.

Upon the plain of Châlons was then to be decided the fate of Europe; the combatants there assembled had been drawn together from the immense tract of country which reaches from the straits of Gibraltar to the Caspian sea. It is impossible in our days to approach the consideration of this contest without bringing to mind that nearly fourteen centuries after this great event, the armies of the same immeasurable line of territory were to be again assembled on the same plain, and under circumstances very similar, for the overthrow of the only individual who has arisen since that day, resembling Attila in his character, in his success, in his mode of acting and his views of universal dominion; that both were defeated, and both came forth again to be the terror of Europe in one more final campaign.

52. A hermit declares him to be the Scourge of God.

On his retrograde march towards Châlons, a circumstance is said to have occurred, which, if it was not, as may be suspected, a politic contrivance of his own, was at least adroitly put forward by Attila, for the purpose of increasing the terror of his name, an object of peculiar importance at the moment of a retreat.

A Christian hermit was brought to him, who had been urgent for admittance to his presence, and addressed him at length, assuring him that God, on account of the iniquities of his people, which he fully detailed, placed the sword in his hand, which, when they should have returned to a sound state, he would resume and give to another. He said to him "You are the scourge of God, for the chastisement of the Christians", and added that he would be unsuccessful in the battle he was about to fight, but that the kingdom would not pass out of his hands.

From this moment Attila appears to have assumed the title of Scourge of God, which accorded with his views of oversetting the Christian religion, and establishing his own right to universal dominion upon the grounds of a heavenly delegation. He had long pretended to be the holder of that sword, which was regarded either as the God itself, or the symbol of the principal God which the Scythian nations worshipped.

The title which he now assumed, appears to have furnished a pretext to insincere Christians, under the specious garb of humility and resignation to the chastisement of the Almighty, to betray into his hands the places which they should have defended; and, in an age so prone to superstition, it is not unlikely that it may have influenced many devout Christians to yield to him without offering any resistance. Attila, having heard the prediction of the hermit, consulted his own soothsayers, of whom there was always a multitude with his army.

According to their custom, they inspected the entrails of cattle, and certain veins which were distinguished upon the bones after they had been scraped, and after due deliberation they announced to him an unfavorable issue of the battle, but consoled him by the assurance that the principal leader of his enemies would perish in the engagement.

Attila is said to have understood that the prediction pointed to Aetius, whose loss would have been irreparable to the Romans. He therefore determined to give battle to the allies at a late hour of the day, that he might reap the advantage awarded to him by the prophecy with as little loss as possible, and that the approach of night might screen his army from the reverse which he had reason to expect. He is said to have proposed a truce which was refused by Aetius. It is not improbable that the predictions of his sooth-sayers may have caused him to hesitate, and he was perhaps desirous of a few more days to collect the forces which he might have left in Belgium.

53. Battle of Châlons.

In the night preceding the great battle, an important collision took place between 90,000 of the Francs on the side of the Romans, and of the Gepidae who formed an important part of the Hunnish army, and many on both sides had fallen. Whatever hesitation Attila might have felt in the first instance, he acted with his usual decision when the hour arrived, which was to decide the fate of Western Europe. The hostile armies lay close to each other on an extensive plain, which stretched 150,000 paces in length, and above 100,000 in breadth.

The forces of Attila were on the left, the Romans on the right of a sloping hill, which either army was desirous of occupying on account of the advantage of the position. Aetius commanded the left wing of the allies, with the troops that were in the service of the emperor. Theodoric with his Goths formed the right, and Sangiban with his Alans was placed in the centre, so surrounded as to prevent his withdrawing himself, since he was regarded with suspicion, and known to be fearful of incurring the vengeance of Attila, and he was probably supported by the Francs.

Attila with his Huns, surrounded by a bodyguard of chosen troops, commanded in the centre of his army. His wings were composed of various subject nations, led by their several kings, amongst whom the Ostrogothic brothers Walamir, Theodemir, and Widimir, were conspicuous, distinguished not only by their valor, but by the nobility of their descent, being joint-heirs of the illustrious race of the Amali.

But the most renowned amongst them was Arderic, who led into the field an innumerable force of Gepidae, and commanded the right wing. Attila placed the greatest confidence in his fidelity, and relied much upon his advice. He shared the favor of the Hun with Walamir, who was the eldest and principal king of the Ostrogoths, and highly valued for his sagacity. Walamir commanded the left wing which was opposed to Theodoric. But Attila was the soul of his army; the numberless kings, who served under his orders, attended like satellites to his nod, observed the least motion of his eye, and were ever prompt to execute his commands.

The battle commenced with a struggle for the possession of the higher ground, which was as yet unoccupied. Attila directed his troops to advance to its summit, but Aetius had anticipated his movement, and, having gained possession of it, by the advantage of the ground easily routed the Huns who were advancing, and drove them down the hill. Attila quickly rallied the Huns, and encouraged them by a harangue, in which he said that he should think it a vain thing to inspirit them by words, as if they were ignorant of their duty, and novices in war, after having vanquished so many nations, and actually subdued the world, if they did not suffer what they had won to be wrested from them. A new leader might resort to, and an inexperienced army might require, such exhortations; but it neither became them to hear, nor him to address to them, words of trite and common encouragement; for to what had they been habituated, if not to warfare? what could be sweeter to brave men than vengeance, the greatest of the gifts of nature?

"Let us therefore", he said, "attack the enemy briskly. The assailants are always the stoutest-hearted. Despise the junction of separate nations; to seek alliances betrays weakness. See even now, before the attack, the enemy are panic-stricken; they seek the elevated places, they take possession of the mounds, and, repenting of their hardihood, they are already desirous of finding fortifications in the open plain. The lightness of the Roman arms is known to you; I will not say that they are overpowered by the first wounds, but by the very dust. While they are assembling in line and locking their shields, do you fight after your own manner with excellent spirit, and despising their array, attack the Alans, overwhelm the Visigoths. We must win the repose of victory by destroying the sinews of war; the limbs drop, when the nerves are cut through, and a body cannot stand when the bones are taken from it. Huns, let your spirits rise; put forth all your skill and all your prowess. Let him, who is wounded, demand of his comrade the death of his antagonist; let him, who is untouched, satiate himself with the slaughter of enemies. No weapons will harm those who are doomed to conquer; those who are to die would be overtaken even in repose by their destiny. Why should fortune have made the Huns victorious over so many nations, unless the glory of this contest had been reserved for them? Who opened the passage of the Maeotian swamp to our ancestors, so many centuries shut up and secret? Who enabled them, when as yet unarmed, to defeat their armed adversaries? An allied assemblage will not be able to resist the countenance of the Huns. I am not deceived; this is the field which so many successes have promised to us. I myself will throw the first darts at the enemy, and if any one of you can endure repose while Attila is fighting, he wants the energy of life".

By such exhortations the wonted spirit of his soldiers was renewed, and well may it be seen, by the tenor of his language, how absolute was his control over the various kings, of whose subjects his army was composed, when he could thus publicly contrast the unity of his own force, with the weakness of an allied confederacy. They rushed impetuously onward, and, though the posture of affairs under the disadvantage of ground was formidable, the presence of Attila prevented any hesitation; they engaged hand to hand with the enemy. The contest was fierce, complicated, immense, and obstinate, to which, according to the assertion of Jornandes, the records of antiquity presented nothing similar. That historian, who wrote about a century after, says that he heard from old men, that a rivulet which traversed the plain was swollen by blood into the appearance of a torrent, and that those, who were tormented by thirst and the fever of their wounds, drank blood from its channel for their refreshment. In the heat of the battle Theodoric riding along the ranks and animating his Visigoths, was knocked off his horse, as it was reported, by the dart of Andages an Ostrogoth in the army of Attila. In the confusion his own cavalry charged over him, and he was trampled to death. It appears that the Ostrogoths, who formed the left wing of the Huns, were overpowered by this charge and gave way, and that the Visigoths advancing beyond the Alans, who were opposed to Attila in the centre, had turned the position of the Huns, and threatened their flank and rear; but, seeing the danger with which he was menaced, Attila immediately fell back upon his camp, which was fenced round by his baggage wagons, behind which the Hunnish archers presented an insurmountable obstacle to the impetuosity of the Gothic cavalry. But the whole army did not retire behind the defenses, and the Huns stood firm until it was dark; for Torismond, the eldest son of Theodoric, who was not by his father's side in the battle, but had been stationed by the wary Aetius near his own person, probably as a surety for the fidelity of Theodoric, and had at the first driven the Huns down the hill in concert with the Romans, being separated from them afterwards, and mistaking in the darkness the Hunnish troops for the main body of the Visigoths, came unawares near the wagons, and fighting valiantly was wounded on the head and knocked off his horse, and being rescued by his soldiers discontinued the attack.

The superstition of the combatants increased the horrors of a nocturnal conflict, and a supernatural voice was supposed to have been heard by either army, which terminated the conflict. While this advantage had been gained at night-fall by the right wing of the allies, which had broken the left and forced the centre of Attila's army to fall back, the left wing under Aetius had been roughly handled by Arderic, and separated from the main body of his forces.

Aetius, ignorant of the success of his right and cut off from all communication with the rest of his army, was in the greatest peril, and fearful that the Visigoths had been overpowered. With difficulty he retreated to his camp, and passed the night under arms, expecting his entrenchments to be attacked by a victorious enemy. A most qualified victory it was, but certainly a victory, for the Visigoths did carry the battle to the very camp of Attila, whose right wing, though successful, did not pursue Aetius to his; but the singular result of this engagement was, that each of the chief commanders passed the night under momentary expectation of an assault from his antagonist. Attila, with the desperate resolution of a pagan, made a vast pyre within the limits of his encampment, which was piled up with harness, and such of the accoutrements of his cavalry, as were not in immediate use, on which he had determined to burn himself with his women and riches, in case his defenses should be stormed, that he might not fall alive into the hands of his enemies, nor any one of them boast of having slain him; but he presented a determined front to the allies, and placed a strong force of armed men and archers in front of the cars, keeping up at the same time an incessant din of warlike instruments to animate his own troops, and alarm those of Aetius by the expectation of an attack.

54. Retreat of the Visigoths.

The dawn discovered to both armies a plain absolutely loaded with the bodies of the slain, and Aetius, perceiving that Attila stood on the defensive, and showed no intention of advancing, became sensible of the successes of the former evening; and, after he had communicated with the Visigoths, it was determined to attempt to reduce Attila by a blockade, as the army of Stilicho had reduced the great host of Radagais near Florence; for the fire of the Hunnish archers was so hot, that they dared not attack him in his position.

But the victorious Theodoric was missing, and no one amongst his troops could account for his disappearance. Torismond and his brother instituted a search for his body, and it was discovered amongst the thickest heaps of the slain. It was borne in sight of the Huns with funereal songs to the camp of the Visigoths, where his obsequies were celebrated with pompous ceremony and loud vociferations, which seemed discordant to the ears of the polished Romans; and Torismond was raised to the estate of a king upon the shield of his forefathers. Having offered to his departed father all the honors, which the customs of his countrymen required, he was ardently desirous of revenging himself on Attila, and would gladly have bearded the lion in his den, but he was not so rash as to attempt an attack with his Visigoths alone; and it was necessary to consult with Aetius. That crafty politician, who appears at every moment of his life to have played a double game, did not consider it for his own advantage to renew the attack. The Huns had sustained such a severe loss of men, that it was not probable that Attila would then renew his attempt either to penetrate into the Roman province, or to conquer the kingdom of the Visigoths. On the other hand, if he should succeed in utterly overpowering the Hun, he dreaded to find a second Alaric in his grandson, who might prove not less formidable to the empire.

His own views were fixed upon the imperial purple, and the report, that he entered into secret negotiations with Attila, after the battle of Châlons, with a view to his own advancement, is probably correct. Being consulted by his young ally, he advised him to forbear from renewing the attack, and to retire with his forces to his own dominions, lest his younger brothers should take advantage of his absence to possess themselves of his throne. With like craftiness, he persuaded Meroveus rather to content himself with what remained to him of the kingdom of Clodion, than to risk the consequence of another engagement, in the hope of recovering the Belgian territory.

The loss of human life in the battle is estimated at about 160,000 souls, and whether we look to the numbers and prowess of the combatants, the immensity of the carnage, or its consequences to the whole of Europe, it was undoubtedly one of the most important battles that were ever fought.

When the retreat of the Visigoths was first announced to Attila, he imagined that it was a crafty device of the enemy to lure him into some rash undertaking, and he remained for some time close in his camp; but when the utter and continued silence of their late position convinced him that they had really withdrawn, his mind was greatly elevated, and all his hopes of obtaining universal dominion were instantly renewed. He was very boastful in his language, and is said to have cried out, as soon as the departure of Torismond was confirmed, "A star is falling before me and the earth trembling. Lo, I am the hammer of the world".

In that singular expression will be recognized an allusion to the hammer of the God Thor, of which the form is known to have been a cross, and in fact nearly identical with that of the mysterious sword which Attila wore, reversing it so that the hilt becomes the mallet and the blade the handle. He met with no further opposition from any part of the allied army, from which it may be pretty surely concluded that Aetius did enter into a secret arrangement with him, which, though suspected, never became public, as Aetius did not communicate it to the Romans. If we may judge from the result, the terms must have been that Attila should not attack the Roman province or kingdom of Tolosa, but should retain his Belgian conquests which were raised into the kingdom of Cameracura for Alberon, and should not be molested by the allies; to which we may suppose that Aetius added private terms to promote his own elevation. It is probable that when, after the decease of Attila, Valentinian caused Aetius to be put to death, he was apprised of his treasonable plans, which were perhaps on the eve of being carried into execution.

55. Sacrifice to the Sword-God. Entrance into Troyes.

In order to remove the impression of a defeat, Attila, having surveyed the field of battle, of which he was ultimately left the master by the retreat of those who had defeated him in a qualified manner, ordered a great sacrifice to be made according to the practice of his nation, to the God Mars, that is to the sword which he wore, and which was the visible personification of the war-god. The fashion of that sacrifice was after this manner. They raised a lofty square structure of faggots, measuring 375 paces on each of its sides, three of which were perpendicular, but the fourth graduated, so that it was easily ascended. In their regular stations such structures were renovated every year by an accumulation of 150 wagon loads of brushwood. On the summit the ancient iron sword, which was symbolical of the war-god, was planted. To that idol sheep and horses were sacrificed.

The sacrificator first made fast a rope round the feet of the animal, and, standing behind it, by pulling the rope threw it down, and thereupon invoking the God, he cast a halter round its neck, and strangled it by twisting the rope with a stick; and without either burning, or cutting, or sprinkling it, he immediately proceeded to skin and cook it. In ancient times, when their state was very rude, and they dwelt in extensive plains where fuel was very rare, they used the bones of the animals for fuel, as the South Americans do at this day, and even the paunch of the animal for a kettle. As soon as the beast was cooked, the sacrificator taking the first share of the flesh and entrails, threw the rest before him. Of their captives they sacrificed one chosen out of each hundred, not in the same manner as the beasts, but having first poured wine on his head, they cut his throat, and received the blood in a vessel, which they afterwards carried up to the summit of the pile, and they emptied the blood upon the sword. They cut off the right shoulder of each man that was thus slaughtered, together with the arm and hand, and cast it into the air; and after the completion of their ceremonies they departed, leaving the limb to lie wherever it happened to have fallen, and the body apart from it Such was the mode in which the ancient Scythians had sacrificed nine hundred years before; such were the rites by which the Huns had celebrated their first successes in Europe, and by which Attila now returned thanksgiving on the plain of Châlons for the retreat of the Christians.

Such was the man, before whom the Christians trembled, and with whom the Arians and some other sectarians are said to have been plotting for the destruction of the Catholics. Ammianus Marcellinus had already testified, that in his time no wild beasts were so blood-thirsty as the various denominations of Christians against each other. Probably more with a view to wipe out the impression of his retreat, and of the check which he had received, than of prosecuting the invasion, he now moved forward again with his whole force, not in the direct line to Orleans, but in a direction which appeared to threaten Orleans, and he advanced against Troyes on the 29th of July. Lupus the bishop of that place, and soon after sanctified, delivered up the town to Attila, and prevailed upon him to spare the place and its inhabitants. He is said to have gone out bareheaded, attended by his clergy and many of the citizens to meet Attila, and to have asked him, who he was that subdued kings, overturned nations, destroyed towns, and reduced everything under his subjection.

Attila replied, "I am the king of the Huns and the scourge of God". To which Lupus answered saying, "Who shall resist the scourge of God, which may rage against whomsoever he will! Come therefore, scourge of my God, proceed whithersoever you will; all things shall obey you, as the minister of the Almighty, without impediment from me".

Attila marched through the town without injuring it, and the Christian legends say that the Huns were smitten with blindness, so that they passed on without seeing anything, a miracle attributed to the sanctity of Lupus. That hypocritical villain received, as the minister of his God, the barbarian whose sword was reeking with the recent immolation of his Christian captives, and he proceeded with Attila to the Rhine, and did not return to his diocese. His panegyrists assert that Attila for the good of his own soul compelled Lupus to accompany him. It is not unlikely that Attila may have thought that such a mock Christian in high dignity might be useful to him, by inducing others to submit, and the bishop probably thought that, after the part he had acted, he was safest under Attila's protection; not having anticipated, when he received the Hun with such honors, that he would immediately afterwards retire from France.

He is eulogized by Sidonius Apollinaris, soon after bishop of Clermont, whose praise is perhaps not very valuable, and whose writings, very different from those of Prudentius, as well as his name, bear the stamp rather of paganism than of genuine Christianity. Attila thence changed the direction of his march and returned to Pannonia. He certainly, however, left an organized force behind to defend the Belgian kingdom of Cameracum against Meroveus, for Alberon and his two brothers continued in possession of it, till they were defeated by the army of Clovis (Louis), and subsequently massacred by him.

Having passed through Troyes, Attila, seeing the people flying to the woods, had compassion on them, and ordered them to return home without fear. A woman with one little girl tied round her neck, two others on a pack-horse, and seven elder daughters accompanying her on foot, cast herself at his feet and supplicated his protection. It was the policy of Attila to treat with general clemency those who threw themselves on his mercy, while he exterminated those who defied him, and he was naturally good-natured, when his ambitious views were not thwarted. He raised up the suppliant lady benignly, and dismissed her with assurances of his favor, and ample gifts to enable her to educate and give marriage portions to her daughters.

56. Eutropia. St. Ursula and the tale of the slaughtered virgins.

The Huns who were left to defend and complete the reduction of Belgium are said to have been commanded by Giulas, who commenced his career by the sack of Rheims, of which the inhabitants had given great offence by harassing the Hunnish army before the battle of Châlons. The citizens in extreme distress crowded round their bishop Nicasius, imploring his advice in the fatal alternative of hopeless resistance, or surrender to the certain vengeance of the barbarians. Nicasius admonished them that the success of Attila was permitted on account of their sins; but that they were destined to brief torments in the hands of the tyrant to obtain salvation and heavenly life. He exhorted them to follow and imitate his example.

His sister Eutropia, a pious virgin of exceeding beauty, seconded his exhortations; and many of the citizens animated by their enthusiastic piety accompanied them to the church of the Virgin Mary, singing hymns and psalms, in the midst of which Nicasius was butchered by the Huns. The beauty of Eutropia excited the desires of the conqueror who had slain her brother, but she is said to have torn out both his eyes, and was slain with all the Christians who had taken refuge in the church. Rheims was demolished, but Attila was not present. Diogenes, bishop of Arras, was also killed by the Huns and the town destroyed. Tongres underwent the same fate, notwithstanding the sanctity and prayers of St. Servatius. Maastricht suffered either before or after the battle of Châlons.

After the destruction of Tongres, the Huns are said to have undertaken the siege of Cologne, which has been rendered famous by the alleged martyrdom of St. Ursula and 11,010 virgins, an absurd fable, which it will be however proper to notice, as the lady has obtained a place in the calendar. If the eyes of the Hunnish general had been extinguished, he could scarcely have commanded in the subsequent operations; supposing them to have been lacerated by Eutropia, it is not improbable that he may have acted very ferociously and butchered many young women at Cologne, but the story of Ursula is utterly absurd, and the name Giulas seems like a corruption of Julius borrowed from an older tale, and was probably not the real name of a Hunnish commander.

Sigebertus, who flourished at the end of the eleventh century, is probably the first writer extant who detailed the story as relating to Ursula. The tale is given with some variation by different authors.

The account of Nicolas Olaus is as follows: Ursula was the only daughter of the king of Britannia; she was courted by Ethereus son of the king of the Angli, who requested her father to betroth her to him, on condition that she should be permitted to travel for three years according to her vow, requiring from Ethereus ten virgins of undoubted chastity for her companions, to each of whom as well as to herself a thousand maidens should be attached. The 11,011 virgins entered the mouth of the Rhine on board eleven large ships, and proceeded to Cologne and Basle, whence they journeyed on foot to Rome, and, having visited all the shrines in that quarter, according to her vow, they returned with Cyriac pope of Rome to Basle and Cologne, where the whole party were intercepted and massacred by the Huns under Giulas.

Gobelin Persona (born AD 1358), in Cosmodrom, fully exposes the absurdity of the story, and shows that there never was such a pope or bishop of Rome, and that such visitations to Rome were unknown at that period. He says the tale was derived from a recluse of Shonaugia about the year 1156; and Pray, trusting to G. Persona, says that Elizabetha Shonaugiensis, in her revelations in the 12th century, first added its present form to the story of the virgins, which is untrue, for she did not even place the event in the age of Attila. It is certain that Ursula's name was in the calendar of saints before the time of Elizabeth, and that she did not invent the tale, because she mentions having seen what she relates in a vision on the day of the feast of the 11,000 holy virgins.

Cardinal Desericius found at Rome an old and imperfect MS. which refers the event to the year 237, saying that Alexander Severus sent Maximin the Thracian from Illyria to repress the Germans near the Rhine. The former being killed, Maximin proclaimed himself emperor. He employed Julius prefect of the Rhine to besiege Cologne, and, through hatred to the Romans, caused the virgins returning from Rome to be massacred by Julius. It states another account to be that when Maximin moved to the siege of Aquileia, where he perished, Julius collected a band of Suni (a people of Germany mentioned by Pliny, Tacitus, and Cluverius), and slew the virgins, and that Suni was afterwards confounded with Hunni, who were called according to the Latin orthography Chuni. The MS. quotes Lampridius and Julius Capitolinus falsely.

Another account in Baronius (Ann. eccles.) refers the tale to the year 381. He says that Gratian having conciliated the Huns, wished that part of them should attack Great Britain with a fleet, and part enter Gaul in concert with the Alans; that Conan, a petty king in Great Britain, accompanied Maximus from thence to Gaul, and persuaded him to locate the British troops in the territory evacuated by the Armoricans, and to send over to Dinoc king of Cornwall for Ursula who was betrothed to Conan, and 11,000 virgins for wives to the soldiers who were to form the new colony; that Gaunus a Hunnish, and Melga a Pictish, pirate intercepted them, and, as they preferred death to the loss of virginity, slew them all. Baronius probably derived the account from Geoffrey of Monmouth, and it originated in the Brut or Chronicle of the kings of Britain, which says that Maximus and Cynan having killed Hymblat king of the Gauls, Maximus gave Armorica to Cynan, who sent to the earl of Cornwall for 11,000 daughters of noble Britons, 60 daughters of foreigners, and servant maids. Their ships were dispersed and some sank. Two were seized by Gwnass and Melwas, the former commander of the Huns, the latter of the Picts, who were at sea with crews in support of Gratian. Another manuscript of the Brut says that Cynan was enamored of the daughter of Dunawd king of Cornwall, and sent for her with a large number of British women. See Roberts, Chron. of the kings of Brit. p. 101, where um-vil-ar-deg is erroneously translated 1100 instead of 11,000. See Walters dict. voc. hundred.

There appears no reason to doubt the veracity of this narrative, which accounts for the subsequent connection between Britany and Cornwall; and it appears by a letter of St Ambrose to Maximus that the Huns were employed at that time by the Roman emperor; and from another it is evident that the Huns had been desired to enter Gaul, but were diverted by Valentinian. Sigebertus in his chronicle says that in 389 Gnamus and Melga were leaders of the Huns and Britons employed by Gratian against Maximus, and laid waste Great Britain, but were driven into Ireland by a detachment sent by Maximus.

The Huns as a nation had certainly no navy or maritime habits, but it is not improbable that, when they overran the North, some of them may have adventured as sea-rovers after the example of the Northmen. Vegnier, Vertot, Dubos, Turner, &c deny the migration of Britons into Armorica in the time of Maximin, and maintain that the first Briton who settled there was one Rhivallon who fled from the encroachments of the Saxons in 513. The Loire is the southern boundary of Britany, and the words of Sidonius Apollinaris who wrote in the 5th century, and says that Euric king of Thoulouse was advised to invade and conquer the Britons situated above the Loire, is decisive as to the error of their assertion. Their king appears to have been Riothamus, to whom a letter addressed by Sidonius is extant, and he is mentioned by Jornandes as Riothimus king of the Britons amongst the Bituriges in France. The upshot of the whole appears to be that when Maximus founded a British colony in Britany in the 4th century, some of the wives or intended brides of the colonists were intercepted by a Hunnish and Pictish pirate in the service of Gratian; that in the following century the general of Attila, having had his eyes lacerated by Eutropia, perhaps butchered some women at Cologne, called Colonia Ubiorum; that Ursula the bride of the prince of the British colony, having been killed by the pirates, had been sanctified as a martyr; and that in the 11th or 12th centuries the stories were confounded, the women who were slain having in both instances belonged to a colony, (Colon ia) and suffered for resisting the incontinency of the Huns.

That such is the real history of this fable appears further from this, that Floras, Ado, and Wandelbert, writers of the 8th and 9th centuries on martyrology, state the murder of the virgins at Cologne, but nothing about Great Britain, Ursula, Ethereus, or any names of virgins or anything concerning a pilgrimage to Rome. That Cologne (Agrippina Colonia Ubiorum) was destroyed by the Huns is affirmed by Sigonius, Herm. Fleinius in vit. SS. ad 21 Oct and Harseus ap. Vales. and others besides the Hungarian writers.

57. Return to Pannonia. Attila advances against Italy.

From Troyes Attila probably returned directly to Pannonia, through either Strasbourg or Basle, continuing his course along the Danube. He passed the ensuing winter at his capital Sicambria, which was perhaps the ancient Buda. It is fabulously stated to have been founded by Antenor the Trojan.

When Attila either built or enlarged Sicambria, he is said to have wished to bestow his own name upon it, and the fatal quarrel between him and his brother is stated to have arisen from a dispute whether it should be called Attila or Budawar. Bleda is by some writers named Buda, and in Scandinavian sagas Buddla is given as the name of the father of Attila, and perhaps it may be considered as having some reference to the name Buddha, the oriental title of Woden or Odin, who seems to have been on some occasions identified with Attila himself in ancient Scandinavian legends. The winter was employed in recruiting his forces, and at the opening of the spring of 453, Attila had under his command a more powerful army, than that with which he had entered Gaul. Early in the season he set this mighty host in motion for the overthrow of Rome. As he mounted on his horse to take the command of this momentous expedition, a crow is said to have perched on his right shoulder, and immediately afterwards to have risen so high into the air, that it could no longer be discerned.

The augury was accepted with joy, and the soldiers anticipated nothing less than the subjugation and plunder of Italy. It will be remembered that the God Odin is fabled to have had two crows or ravens which flew every day round the world to do his missions, and returned at evening to his heavenly mansion; nor were these messengers unknown to the Greek and Roman mythology. Plutarch relates that two crows were sent out by Jupiter, one to the east, the other to the west, and, having flown round the world, met at Delphi. Livy writes that when Valerius, hence called Corvinus, was engaged in contest with a powerful Gaul, a crow lighted on his helmet, and gave him the victory by assailing the eyes of his antagonist; and we know from Prudentius that this was one of the Delphic crows, sacred to Apollo.

It is stated by Strabo that when Alexander the Great was in danger of perishing amidst the sands of the desert, on his way from Parsetonium to the temple of Jupiter Ammon, he was delivered by the guidance of two crows; nor will it be forgotten that ravens brought food to Elijah. With these recollections it seems not improbable that Attila may have practised some imposture in the sight of his army, or at least that such a tale was purposely circulated amongst his followers, to promote the superstitious belief of a communication having been made to him by the Deity. There is much discrepancy in the various accounts of the route by which he entered Italy, but from the enormous bulk of his army it is probable that they may all be founded in truth, and that his army advanced in several columns which were to reunite after having passed the Alps.

The Byzantine emperor Marcian, who had the administration of the provinces on the northwest of the Adriatic, had left their numerous towns ungarrisoned. Attila crossed the Drave and the Save, and the whole of Styria, Carinthia, Illyria, and Dalmatia, was overrun by his forces without any serious opposition. Aetius, who commanded the armies of Rome, whether from treasonable views, or because Valentinian kept the main forces of the empire for the immediate defence of Rome, whither he had withdrawn from Ravenna upon the alarm of an approaching invasion, certainly made no attempt to oppose the progress of the great antagonist whom he had so lately discomfited on the plain of Châlons; but the whole tenor of his life seems to mark that he must have been consulting his own personal aggrandizement, and utterly disregarding the interests of his country.

We may figure to ourselves the reminiscences of that great and dissembling commander, while, stretching his hopes to the acquisition of power exceeding that of the mightiest emperors, he lay in purposed inactivity before Rome, awaiting the effects of intemperance and disorganization on the force of Attila, and distraction and imbecility on the imperial counsels. We may fancy him bringing to mind the early instructions of his Scythian father, and of his mother who was descended from one of the most illustrious families of Latium; the youthful energy which had led him to excel in every exercise of the field or forest; his first and early military achievements; his sojourn as a hostage in the court of Alaric, and afterwards of Rhuas the Hunnish monarch; the hypocrisy with which he had pretended to embrace Christianity, while his heart was imbued with the leaven of paganism; his initiation of his son Carpileo into all the orgies of idolatry in the capital of Attila; his abode in the palace of John the usurper; his advance at the head of a Hunnish army towards Ravenna, the consternation with which he heard of the sudden destruction of John, and the art with which he made his peace with Valentinian; the military titles which were the reward of his treason, extorted from his imbecile rulers; his command in Gaul, where in three campaigns he rescued Aries from the Visigoths, the Rhine from Clodion, and overwhelmed the Juthungians of Bavaria; the treachery by which he had compromised Boniface, and the ruin he brought thereby on the Roman authority in Africa; his personal conflict with Boniface, and mortification at the only defeat he suffered in his life, and the malignant joy with which he heard of the subsequent death of his rival; his flight from the arm of justice to Ms pagan ally, and the authority which he again obtained through the influence of the enemies of his country; his further successes in Gaul and Burgundy; the art with which he reconciled Theodoric to the Roman arms; the energy with which he inspired his allies; the mighty conflict of Châlons; the skill with which he diverted Torismond from avenging his father, and persuaded Meroveus to remain content with the Parisian kingdom; his secret negotiations with Attila, and all the vast and daring projects which had been since fermenting in his mind. If we place this picture before us, we shall probably have filled up the outline of historical truth with no unreal imaginations.

The heart sickens, when we bring to mind the praises lavished by Gibbon upon this evil man, the outbreaking of whose treachery was probably anticipated by the jealousy of his roaster, and his sudden destruction. The existence of a coin bearing the superscription Flavius Aetius imperator, gives reason to suspect that he had even committed an overt act of treason before he was cut short by Valentinian.

58. Enters Carnia.

The defence of the Julian Alps, through which the Huns were preparing to enter Italy, was entrusted to a small number of Visigothic auxiliaries under Alaric and Antal or Athal. Emona a flourishing town at the foot of the Alps was evacuated by its inhabitants on the approach of the invaders, by whom it was so completely destroyed, that no author recognizes its existence after that period. The Roman auxiliaries delayed the advance of Attila a little through the Goritian forest; but, after many conflicts, they were forced to abandon the mountain passes, and multitudes of barbarians poured through them with overwhelming impetuosity on the delightful district of Forum Julii. On the first alarm of an intended invasion, Valentinian had taken measures to put the important city of Aquileia in a state to resist the advance of the enemy. About the year 190 before the birth of Christ, the Gauls, having entered Carnia from Germany, had founded a city near the site of Aquileia, which was soon destroyed by the Romans. The Istri invaded the province four years after, whereupon the senate determined to build a town for the defence of the neighboring territory, and in the year 181 before Christ Aquileia was founded by a colony from Rome. Augustus Caesar adorned Aquileia with temples and theatres, fortified the harbor, and paved the roads. He increased its circuit to twelve miles, or, as some say, to fifteen.

The remains of a double wall were to be seen in tolerable preservation in the 17th century, running directly east, eleven miles in length, like two parallel lines, composed of stones piled up, but not cemented by any kind of mortar. Aquileia stood on the banks and at the mouth of the river Natissa, which washed a large part of its wall. Sabellicus supposes that the name of the Sontius was lost after its junction with the Natissa, (whereas on the contrary the modern name of the Natisone is lost in the Isonzo) or else that the Natissa did not in ancient times fall into the Sontius, or that a stream flowed by a subterraneous channel out of the Natissa into the sea, because both Pliny and Strabo mention the mouth of the Natissa.

He adds that in his time only a church of the Virgin Mary, and the huts of a few peasants and fishermen remained on the site of Aquileia; but that many monuments, public ways, magnificent and sumptuous paved roads, aqueducts, sepulchers, and pavements, were still extant, by which the great size and distinguished appearance of the ancient town might be easily ascertained. The territory of Aquileia was called Forum Julii and also Carnia. The Carnians were a people inhabiting the mountains, where they led a pastoral life, their country being too rugged for tillage. In the year of our Lord 167 the physician Galen followed M. Aurelius and L. Commodus to Aquileia, and wrote his commentaries there.

In 361 in the reign of Julian his general Immon besieged Aquileia, and finding that the citizens derived great advantage from the river as a defence and means of obtaining provisions, he discontinued the siege, and employed his army by an immense exertion to excavate a new bed for the river, and conduct it to the sea at a considerable distance from the town. The inhabitants were however supplied by plenty of cisterns and wells, and did not suffer from the loss of water. Aquileia underwent another siege subsequently, when Maximin was discomfited before its walls and put to death by his own troops.

Herodian, who gives an account of this siege, states that Aquileia was a city of the first magnitude, with an abundant population, being situated on the seashore in front of all the Illyrian nations, as the emporium of Italy, delivering to navigators the produce of the continent brought down by land or by the rivers, and furnishing seaborne necessaries, especially wine, to the upper countries, which were less fertile than the southern provinces from severity of climate.

59. Aquileia.

Immediately after crossing the Alps, Attila routed and utterly annihilated the Roman force which was opposed to him in the neighborhood of Tergeste, the modern Trieste, especially the cavalry under Forestus the distinguished ruler of Atestia, the modern Este, and other Italian troops which had been placed there by Menapus the governor of Aquileia to oppose his progress. The Huns then crossed the Sontius, and directed their whole might against Aquileia, which was at that time one of the fairest and most flourishing cities in the world, but was destined to be trampled under the relentless foot of Attila, and to become a desolation and a thing obliterated from the earth. Belenus, Felenus, or Belis had been the tutelary God of Aquileia, and, although the population was now at least nominally Christian, he was still held in great veneration as a guardian saint, if not an actual Deity. Herodian states that, when Maximin was engaged in the fruitless siege of Aquileia, before which he lost his life by the hands of his own soldiers, the besieged were encouraged by the oracles of their peculiar or provincial God Belin, or, if the word be inflected, Belis, whom they worshipped most religiously, and considered to be Apollo. The soldiers of Maximin affirmed that they beheld the likeness of the God in the air, fighting for the town, either superstitiously fancying that they saw something unusual, or making use of the fable to cover their own unwillingness.

Julius Capitolinus says that the discomfiture of Maximin was fortold by the augurs of the God Belenus, who is mentioned also by Ausonius. G. F. Palladio says that, when Maxentius was patriarch, about the year 841, a church and monastery of Benedictine monks was built out of the ruins of the temple of the false God of the province named Bellenus, not far from Aquileia, and was named L'Abbatia della Belligna, but was afterwards abandoned on account of malaria. The name given to the monastery and derived from that of the pagan God, out of the ruins of whose temple it was constructed, is very deserving of notice.

In the same manner the temple of Flora at Brescia became the chapel of St Floranus. These are amongst the numerous instances of the manner in which the Christians compounded with the pagans, not really converting them, but permitting the worship of their favorite idol under the licensed character of a saint. This baneful practice became a main source of the corruption of the church of Rome.

The Christianity of the Aquileians must have continued in a very unsettled state, for Stephen the patriarch in 517 was an Arian, and the epitaph of Elias the patriarch, who removed the see of Aquileia to Grado, states him to have been a Manichaean. Palladius gives eight inscriptions in which Belenus is named. The last is Apollini Beleno C. Aquileien. felix .... He adds that the church of St Felix the martyr stands where the temple of Belenus was; that the natives do not call it Felix, but Felus (non Felicem sed Felum) with an evident allusion, as he observes, to the ancient name of the God. He adds that there is another more certain reminiscence of Belenus, because there still exists a noble abbey of which the tutelary saint is called St. Martin, (and be it recollected that in Latin these saints were actually called Divi) but is universally called Belenus for no other reason than the recollection of the idol, which after so many centuries could not be extinguished by any rites of true religion. In fact it was the corrupt impropriety of those rites, which, by attributing divinity to the saint, nourished and appeared to justify the reminiscence of the idol. Palladius adds that in the first age of Christianity the Aquileians did not desist from worshipping Belenus with magnificent sacrifices, and were so prone to that superstition, that those who were initiated in it were a great obstacle to the spread of Christianity.

Sir John Reresby, who travelled in the time of Cromwell, speaking of Venice says: "The palace of the patriarchs is one of the first, where we saw some ancient statues of the Roman Gods, as of Bacchus, Mercury, Pallas, Venus, and others; as also some little couches or beds on which the Romans used to lie when they made feasts in honour of their Gods. Upon these are engraved certain characters, signifying vows made to the God Bellinus, formerly in great repute amongst the Aquileians, from whom these were taken with many other antiquities, at the razing of one of their chief cities and a Roman colony by Attila king of the Huns".

This is a curious confirmation of the account given by Sabellicus and H. Palladium that Menapus governor of Aquileia removed the valuables and furniture of the town to the Venetian isle of Gradus before he evacuated it, written by a person who does not appear to have known that Aquileia itself had been sacked by Attila. Joannes Candidas, a lawyer of Venice, whose work was published in 1521, seven years after that of Sabellicus, discredits the accounts of Menapus and Oricus, but without any reason assigned, probably from indiscriminate disgust at the Atestine forgeries. H. Palladius gives a remarkable inscription found at Aquileia, and dated a few years before its destruction. Januarius who thus forewarned the inhabitants of the city of its approaching destruction by the scourge of God was patriarch before Nicetas, and died in 452 before the accomplishment of the visitation he foresaw.

60. Construction of Hunnium.

On the approach of the enemy Menapus ordered a simultaneous sally from two gates of the town, and slew many of the Huns who had advanced incautiously, and put their van to flight. The conflict was continued for many hours, when he was at last forced to give way before the increasing numbers of the enemy, and retreated safely into the town.

Attila fortified his encampment, and on the following day accompanied by a few followers is said to have reconnoitered the town. He had almost reached the river, when Menapus suddenly attacked him from the rear. Attila with difficulty escaped, wounded, and baring lost the ornament of his helmet, and the greater part, if not the whole, of his attendants. After this hazardous encounter he became more cautious, acted more through the agency of his generals, and exposed himself less to personal danger.

According to another account, he had been in the habit of going his rounds alone and disguised, to observe the most assailable points of the city, and having been induced by the apparent silence and loneliness of the wall to approach nearer than usual, he was surprised by a body of armed men, who, having observed him, had sallied through a sewer under the walls, not knowing him to be the great king, but desirous of extorting from a hostile spy the plans of the enemy, and learning what hopes they entertained of capturing the town.

They surrounded him, therefore, wishing to take him alive. He placed his back against a steep bank, so that he could only be assailed in front, and defended himself; but finding the Aquileians, who were not desirous of killing him, remiss in the attack, he suddenly sprang forward with a loud shout and slew two of them, and immediately vaulting over the wall of some buildings near the town, he escaped to his own troops. Those, who bad surrounded him, reported that, while he was looking round and collecting his strength for the assault, the appearance of his eyes was in a manner celestial, and sparks of fire glanced from them, like the energy attributed by heathen writers to the eyes of their Gods. The same anecdote is related by another historian, who states that he was on horseback, and that the circumstance took place near the end of the siege, the day before he observed the departure of the stork. He also speaks of the sparks emitted from his eyes, and says that when two of the assailants had been slain by him, the rest were daunted and suffered him to depart.

Menapus was a man of great activity and valor; he did not permit the Huns to enjoy a moment of rest by day or night, sometimes attacking them by surprise, sometimes openly, intercepting their foragers, capturing their stragglers, and carrying slaughter and tumult into their quarters by night Attila at the commencement of the siege had no instruments for taking towns with him except ladders, either because his people were not skilful in the construction of engines, or because he preferred, through excess of pride, to rely on their personal exertions. A desperate attack was however made by the Huns with ladders, which was repelled by the garrison, who threw stones, fire, and boiling water, on the assailants; Menapus everywhere exerting himself, exhorting and exciting his troops, rewarding valor and punishing remissness. After a great loss of men, Attila was forced to discontinue the assault, but it was renewed day after day with no better success, till at last the Huns found it necessary to make regular and scientific approaches, throwing up a bank and constructing vineo, which at that time were the usual protection of besiegers. At this period of the siege it is probable that Attila undertook the great work at Udine, which was at first called Hunnium, and afterwards Utinum, as a place of safety for his sick and wounded, and a strong depot, whenever he might advance into Italy. The conical hill which he raised and fortified, remains to this day an imperishable monument of the immensity of his resources.

All writers concerning it agree that it was fortified by Attila during the siege, having been perhaps originally strengthened by Julius Caesar. H. Palladium gives an ample account of it to the following effect Attila raised it up and fortified it as a safe post during the siege, and a point of support for his future operations. During the beleaguerment of Aquileia, the concourse to Hunnium had been so great, that many had built themselves houses of wood and stone along the way to Aquileia. Attila feared that a sally from thence might overpower these defenseless houses, and he abstained from pressing the siege for a few days, while he marked out the site of a town, and surrounded it with a strong rampart and gates protected by towers. After the capture of Aquileia he built a wall on the new rampart, and raised the mound of the Julian fortress, not only the slaves and captives, but all the soldiers, bringing earth in the cavity of their shields, till it was sufficiently increased. H. Palladius had an opportunity of verifying this account, the earth having been excavated to make a tank, when the artificial nature of one side of the mound was evident, from the admixture of worked stones and fragments of tiles with the earth, and also by the discovery of an old helmet; whereas the other side of the mound consisted of dry rock.

61. Capture of Aquileia.

Having thus raised a secure defence for his own troops against the destructive sallies of the garrison, Attila pressed the siege with vigour. At the northern angle of the tower stood a tower of great antiquity, which, being occupied by a strong force, very much molested Attila. Menapus had strengthened its fortifications, and made a wall and ditch in front of it. It was a great object to Attila to gain possession of this outwork, because it commanded the whole town He therefore approached his works to it, and filled the ditch with earth and stones, and tried by his archery to drive the Aquileians from the walls, while he sent light troops across the ditch to break down the wall with hatchets. Having succeeded in clearing the walls by incessant vollies of arrows, they overleaped the fosse, singing barbarian omens of victory. Menapus came immediately to the relief of the tower, and hot iron, molten lead, and blazing pitch, were thrown upon the Huns. Attila goaded on fresh troops to the attack, compelling them not only by words of command, but by the sword, to advance to certain death. But at length they gained a footing on the inner side of the fosse, and began to destroy the wall, where the mortar of the new works was not perfectly hardened, and a narrow breach was made.

Menapus singly resisted in the breach, and sallied through it, followed by a great power of Aquileians, and they forced their way even to Attila himself through the flying enemy, throwing torches and firebrands amongst them. Oricus brother of the governor sallied at the same time through the nearest gate with the Roman cavalry, and made great havoc amongst the enemy, killing all stragglers, and increasing the disorder of the discomfited Huns. Attila immediately ordered his own cavalry to advance, and charged at their head. After a severe conflict near the villa of Mencetius, Oricus was either killed or mortally wounded, and his followers nearly all cut off.

Menapus, wounded, returned through the breach in the outer wall, and some of the Huns forced their way in, but their comrades were beat off by the engines of the garrison, and he got safe into the town. Night succeeded, and the Huns continued to sap the foundations of the tower, but, being only protected by their shields, they were at last forced to fall back with great loss of men. The Aquileians however had sacrificed their whole cavalry and its leader, a loss which outweighed all the previous slaughter of the enemy, and the town was become ruinous and almost untenable. Forestus and many other valiant men had fallen in its defence.

Menapus, therefore, despairing of successful resistance, as the army of Aetius remained inactive behind the Po, and no hopes of relief were held out to him, sent by night the children and women, and the wounded men to the nearest island, Gradus, with the patriarch Nicetas and the church utensils, being confident that the barbarians, who were unskilled in navigation, would not pursue their enemies by sea. He then attempted to repair the fortifications of the town and the wall in front of it.

The third month was now far spent, since Attila had commenced operations against Aquileia, and yet there was no certain prospect of taking the town. His troops murmured, and began to talk of raising the siege, when he observed a stork remove its young from the long contested tower. Thereupon he turned to his soldiers, and, auguring its speedy fell from that circumstance, he exhorted them to make a most vigorous attack upon it. Having been undermined and shaken before, it was at last beat out of the perpendicular by the immense stones thrown by the engines which he had caused to be constructed. It fell in the night time with a tremendous crash, which made the whole population start out of their beds; and, if Attila had immediately attacked the city, he might have taken it in the first moment of confusion.

The obscurity of the night and the ignorance of the Huns as to the actual state of the defenses gave the besieged a short respite, and Menapus quickly constructed an inner fortification with mud and stones, but he was aware that such a defence could not hold out long. At day break, Attila, having seen the state of things, made a bloody attack, and gained possession of the ruins of the tower; and, having driven the Aquileians behind the old wall, he began to strengthen the post, intending to use it for offensive operations against the town. Menapus now despaired of making good the defence of Aquileia; provisions were beginning to fail, and Valentinian had abandoned the outfit of a fleet which he had ordered to be equipped at Ravenna at the commencement of the siege. The governor therefore removed the greater part of his people to Gradus during the night, and placed statues or figures on the walls to look like sentinels, and prevent the enemy from noticing the evacuation of the city by the garrison.

When the day broke, the Huns at first wondered at the unusual silence, but at length observing birds alight on some of the figures, they perceived that the fortifications were abandoned. They immediately forced their way through the new wall, and killed all the men, children, and aged women, who were still remaining in the town; the younger women found in it were reserved for the embraces of the conquerors. Two matrons of high rank, and distinguished for beauty and chastity, having lost their husbands during the siege, had continued day and night mourning over their tombs, and refused to leave them, when the town was evacuated. Their names were Digna and Honoria. When the defences were stormed, to escape the incontinency of the Huns, Digna ascended an adjoining tower, which stood beside the river, and, having veiled her head, she threw herself into it and perished. Honoria, having thrown her arms round the stone sepulcher in which the remains of her husband were interred, clung to it with such perseverance, that she could not be dragged from it, till slain by the swords of the enemy. Thus fell Aquileia, 633 years after its foundation, perhaps the greatest town in the West after Rome.

Almost all the writers, who mention its overthrow, say that it was completely burnt and demolished, so that the barbarians seemed desirous of obliterating every vestige of its existence, but many circumstances contradict that assertion, which has been hastily adopted by modern historians. Aquileia is frequently mentioned as existing after the departure of Attila, and it is certain that the patriarchs continued to dwell there till the time of the invasion of the Lombards, from whom the last calamity of the town proceeded. Justinian, long after the time of Attila, calls Aquileia the greatest of all the cities of the West, as if it were still existing. Many particulars indeed are known concerning Aquileia, down to the period of the removal of the see. Nicetas, the patriarch, returned from Gradus, after the retreat of Attila, and exerted himself to restore the church and the town.

The fugitives began to reassemble from different quarters, and many of them, having been supposed to have died in the war, found their wives provided with other husbands. This led to a correspondence between Nicetas and Pope Leo, the patriarch complaining that many of the women had remarried, knowing that their husbands were in captivity, and not expecting them to return. Leo exculpated the women who really believed their husbands to be dead, and condemned the others as guilty of adultery, but he ordered all to return to their first husbands under pain of excommunication. He directed those who had been baptized by heretics, not having been before baptized, to be confirmed by imposition of hands as having taken the form of baptism without the sanctification, but he forbad rebaptism. The heretics alluded to were the Sabellians and Arians, of whom there were many in the army of Attila, and who appear to have made common cause with the pagans. The whole letter of Leo is extant, and proves that Nicetas did not fall, as has been asserted, in the siege. He died about the year 463, and his statue and epitaph were placed in the patriarchal hall at Udine.

62. Surrender of Ravenna. Marullus the Calabrian poet.

During the siege detachments from the army of Attila carried devastation far and wide in the adjoining territory, and treason was at work to betray into his hands several of the cities of Italy. Treviso, then Tarvisium, is said to have been yielded to the Huns through the means of its bishop Helinundus, who was probably inclined to the Arians, and of Araicus Tempestas, and Verona to have been given up by Diatheric or Theodoric, who has been celebrated in various Scandinavian and German romances under the name of Thidrek of Bern, meaning Verona, and has been much confounded with Theodoric the great, afterwards king of Italy, who was not then born. After the demolition of Aquileia, Attila marched immediately against Concordia, a flourishing town, of which the ruler Janus (who has become the hero of an Italian, perhaps originally a Provencal, romance) had probably molested him during the siege. Janus, with his wife Ariadne, fled to the nearest islands, and the conqueror entered and annihilated the deserted city. One church, that of St Stephen, and a few cottages were the only remains of Concordia at the end of the 15th century.

Attila next exterminated Altinum. Patavium (Padua), Cremona, Vincentia (Vicenza), Mediolanum (Milan), Brixia (Brescia), and Bergomum (Bergamo), were successively captured. The fugitives from Aquileia had established themselves in the isle of Gradua, the Concordians fled to Crapulse, afterwards Caorli, the Altinates to Torcellum, Maiorbium, and Amorianum, and the Paduans to Rivus altus, which is now nearly the centre of Venice, and is recognized in the modern name of the Rialto.

The foundations of the bright city of the waters was then laid, upon the sedgy islands that fringed the Adriatic, by the refugees from the various towns of Italy that were dismantled by the barbarian. Valentinian had fled from his palace at Ravenna to the protection of the eternal city, and Attila, while besieging Padua, or at a later period of his progress, is said to have received John the Arian bishop of Ravenna, who came with hus clergy in white robes to solicit his mercy for their town and its population, and perhaps to offer him the assistance of the Arians to subjugate all Italy without a conflict, if he would adopt their faith. He is said to have answered that he would spare the town, but would throw down their gates and trample them under the feet of his cavalry, that the inhabitants might not in their vanity imagine their own strength to have been the cause of their preservation.

On his march to Concordia, Attila is said to have met some mountebanks, who, in the hope of obtaining money, jumped with singular skill and agility amongst some swords which were artfully arranged. Thinking the employment despicable for men who had evidently sufficient bodily power and activity to use the sword efficiently in warfare, he ordered them to be covered with armour and to imitate him in vaulting on horseback with the weight of metal on them, which they proved unable to perform; neither could they bend the bow properly, nor fix the arrow in the string. He therefore ordered their well-fed bodies to be reduced by spare diet and exercise, and enrolled them amongst his recruits.

After the capture of Padua, a distinguished poet named Marullus the Calabrian, and who was probably the same person whose poem detailing the latter part of the siege of Troy which had been "left untold by the blind bard of Greece", has descended to us under the name of Quintus Calaber, recited a poem in his praise, which gave him such offence, because it referred his origin to the gods of Greece and Rome, that he ordered it to be burnt and the poet put to death, but he remitted the latter part of the sentence. This anecdote, which was probably extracted from the MS. of Priscus, has been misunderstood by those who imagined from it that he repudiated divine honors, whereas the offence was the connecting him with a worship he detested, and with Bacchus or some other deity of the Pelasgians. Herodotus relates that Scylas, king of the Scythians, was beheaded by his own subjects in Borysthenes, and his palace, which was adorned with marble sphinxes and gryphons, fulminated and burnt by the god of the Scythians, because he adopted the Bacchic rites, which were held in abhorrence amongst them. That furnishes an explanation to the indignation of Attila.

63. Florence. Brescia.

During the attack of Florence, a statue of the god Mars, which notwithstanding the edict of Caesar still occupied an elevated station in the town, having been, however, removed from the temple which was dedicated to St. John, fell into the Arno, probably knocked down by the engines of the besiegers. At Vincentia Attila met with a stout resistance, and, finding his men hesitate, he leaped into the fosse, and wading through the water, which was breast-deep, led them to the assault, and was the first who scaled the rampart. But at Brixia he met with more dangerous opposition, and received a wound in the hand, which induced him to consign that city to more complete destruction than the rest of the conquered places. Yet Brixia was a town in which paganism appears to have lingered particularly. The temple of Flora had been converted into a church dedicated to St Floranus, to accommodate the heathens who adhered to their tutelary divinity, furnishing, like the dedication of the temple of Belis, or Felus, to St. Felix at Aquileia, one of the many instances in which the Church of Rome compromised with the pagans, whom it admitted within its pale without really converting them from idolatry, thus laying the foundation of its own corruption; but, in the Triumpline valley hard by, the iron statue of the god Tyllinus had escaped amidst the general destruction of idols, and remained after the days of Attila. Milan submitted to the conqueror, and a curious anecdote is related m a fragment of Priscus, for the preservation of which we are indebted to his having used an uncommon word for a bag, which caused it to be quoted by the lexicographer Suidas. Attila having observed in Milan a picture of the Roman emperors seated upon a throne of gold, and Scythians prostrate before them, ordered himself to be painted on a throne, and the Roman emperors bearing sacks on their shoulders and pouring out gold from them at his feet. After inflicting this lesson upon the pride of the Caesars he continued his victorious career, plundering Ticinum (Pavia), Mantua, Placentia, Parma, and Ferrara, and, as Jornandes asserts, demolished almost all Italy, which gives some color to the improbable assertion of the Hungarian writers, that he despatched his general Zowar to ravage Apulia, Calabria, and the whole coast of the Adriatic, destroying a town named Catona, as having been founded by Cato. Geminianus, bishop of Mutina (Modena), afterwards sanctified, is said to have played the same game as Lupus and John of Ravenna, and by submission to have conciliated the favor of the invader and saved the town. Attila is particularly stated to have laid waste Emilia (which must mean the country traversed by the via Emilia, between Aquileia and Rimini, Pisa and Tortona) and Marchia, which has been explained to signify the territory of Bergamo, but was in truth used to designate the March of Ancona. Ferrara is said to have been destroyed, though, perhaps, at an earlier period of the campaign.

64. Embassy from Rome.

Thus far had Attila proceeded without meeting any material obstacle after the reduction of Aquileia, but Aetius had probably a considerable force under his command for the protection of Rome, and, since the Huns had crossed the Po, he had not ceased to hang upon their flanks, and to take every opportunity of cutting off their stragglers. A course of desultory victories and continual plunder had probably contributed to relax the discipline and diminish the numbers of the army of Attila. He deliberated whether or not to proceed against Rome, and such deliberations generally end by the adoption of the weaker counsel.

Evil forebodings had become prevalent amongst his vassal kings, who represented to him that Alaric had not long survived the invasion and plunder of the Romulean capital, and the mind of Attila appears at that time to have been influenced by a vague superstitious apprehension. He halted, as the later authorities assert near the confluence of the Mincio and the Po, but it has been presumed from the relation of Jornandes who names the place Acroventus Mambuleius, where the Mincio is forded by travelers, that it must have been where the great Roman road crossed the river at Ardelica, the modern Peschiera, near the point where it issues from the Benacus or Lago di Garda, close to the farm of Virgil, and the Sirmian peninsula of Catullus. It is however by no means improbable that the river might have been forded at some place to the south of Mantua, though the opinion of Maffei has led to the supposition that the place designated was close to Peschiera. Governolo, near the confluence of the Mincio and the Po, is a much more probable situation for the halt of Attila, after having ravaged the southern banks of the Po; for if he had actually fallen back as far as the Benacus before he received the embassy, he must have previously abandoned the prosecution of his enterprise, which is not even surmised by any writer on the subject.

While he was hesitating, whether to advance and attempt the complete subjugation of Rome, or to give way to the forebodings of his advisers, Zowar is said to have returned with great plunder from the coast of the Adriatic, and at the same moment an embassy from Valentinian, who had despatched Leo the pope or bishop of Rome, Avienus a man of consular dignity, and the praetorian prefect Trigetius, arrived at the camp of Attila. Leo is stated by his biographer and some other writers to have thrown himself at the feet of Attila, and to have delivered a speech of the most abject and unconditional submission. He is made to say, after the manner of Lupus, that evil men had felt his scourge, and to pray that the suppliants who addressed him might feel his clemency.

That the senate and Roman people, once conquerors of the world, but now defeated, humbly asked pardon and safety from Attila the king of kings; that nothing amid the exuberant glory of his great actions, could have befallen him more conducive to the present luster of his name or to its future celebrity, than that the people, before whose feet all nations and kings had lain prostrate, should now be suppliant before his. That he had subdued the whole world, since it had been granted to him to overthrow the Romans, who had conquered all other nations. That they prayed him who had subdued all things to subdue himself; that, as he had surpassed the summit of human glory, nothing could render him more like to Almighty God, than to will that security should be extended through his protection to the many whom he had subdued.

The letters however of Leo, which are extant, upon various subjects chiefly connected with church discipline, seem to testify a right-judging and upright mind, and render it very improbable that he should have debased himself and the government which he then represented by such mean and contemptible adulation. Whether he addressed the mighty Hun in the language of abject submission, or strove to conciliate him by a more rational and dignified appeal, he was completely successful in obtaining the object of his mission.

The king is said to have stood silent and astonished, moved by veneration at the appearance, and affected by the tears, of the pontiff; and, when he was afterwards questioned by his vassals, why he had conceded so much to the entreaties of Leo, to have answered that he did not reverence him, but had seen another man in sacerdotal raiment, more august in form and venerable from his grey hairs, who held a drawn sword, and threatened him with instant death, unless he granted everything that Leo demanded. The vision was reputed to be that of St Peter, and according to Nicolas Olaus he saw two figures, who were reported to have been St. Paul and St Peter.

This celebrated anecdote, the memory of which is said to have been made illustrious by the works of Raphael and Algarve, is to be looked upon as an ecclesiastical fiction, but Attila seems to have been alarmed by a superstitious dread of the fate which overtook Alaric speedily after the subjugation of Rome. A joke is related as having been prevalent against Attila amongst his followers, founded on the names of the two bishops Lupus and Leo, that as in Gaul he had yielded to the wolf, he now gave way before the lion. He had probably more weighty reasons for his retreat, than the venerable aspect of the lion, the visions of the apostles, or the fate of the Gothic conqueror. His army was enervated by the sack of the Italian towns, and a grievous pestilence had thinned its ranks; the devastation of the country had rendered it difficult to obtain subsistence, and his troops were suffering from famine, as well as disease; the recollection of Radagais, who had not long before in the plenitude of his power been starved into unconditional surrender on the heights of Faesulae, may have furnished him with rational grounds of apprehension, while the army of Aetius, fresh and unbroken, was hanging upon his skirts, intercepting his foragers, cutting off his stragglers, and watching opportunity to inflict some more important injury.

An ample donation of gold, according to the base practice of that period, was probably added to the causes which induced Attila to forego for that season at least the attack of Rome; and he consented to withdraw his forces, threatening however that he would return in the ensuing spring to inflict the most determined vengeance on the Romans, unless Honoria and her portion of the imperial inheritance were conceded to him. Cassiodorius and Carpileo probably transacted the details of the treaty after the first audience of the ambassadors.

Theodoric king of Italy, in a rescript to the Roman senate, announcing the elevation of M. A. Cassiodorius to the patriciate, asserts that the conclusion of the peace was mainly attributable to the skill and intrepidity of the elder Cassiodorius his father. He speaks in high praise of him, saying that his mental qualities were equal to those of Aetius, and that on account of his wisdom and glorious exertions on behalf of the state he was associated with that distinguished commander, and was therefore deputed with Carpileo son of Aetius to "Attila the armipotent". "Fearless (continues Theodoric) he beheld the man who was dreaded by the empire; confiding in the truth he disregarded his terrible and threatening countenance. He found the king haughty, but left him appeased; and so completely overthrew his calumnious allegations by the force of truth, that he disposed him to seek conciliation, whose interest was not to be at peace with a state so wealthy. By his firmness he raised up the timid party, nor could those be looked upon as faint-hearted, who were defended by such fearless negotiators. He returned with a treaty, which the nation had despaired of obtaining". Theodoric bears no mean testimony to the magnanimity of Attila, when he asserts, that the truth spoken by a foe could disarm him in the full career of his hostility. Cassiodorius, to whom we are indebted for the preservation of Theodoric's account of his father's distinguished ability in conducting the negotiation, says in his chronicle that pope Leo made the peace under the direction of Valentinian.

65. Honoria.Retreat of Attila.

Whether or not Honoria was afterwards delivered up to Attila is a point that admits of doubt, though no mention of her having been given to him is made by the Roman writers; but the Hungarians speak of a son Chaba borne to him by Honoria after his death. Nothing is recorded concerning her after this period, and she most probably died in prison, unless, having been sent to him, she finished her life amongst the heathens.

She was not amongst the ladies of the imperial family whom Genseric afterwards carried off from the sack of Rome to Africa. The steps which had been taken on the discovery of the correspondence of Honoria with Attila are buried in oblivion with the lost work of Priscus, but the expression of Jornandes that Attila asserted that Honoria had done (or, strictly, admitted) nothing which should disqualify her from marrying him, induces me to believe that she was immediately compelled to undergo a mock ceremony of marriage, probably never consummated, for the purpose of preventing her union with him.

A medal has been preserved, and engraved by Angeloni, in which she bears the title of Augusta, which was perhaps struck at this time to appease and gratify Attila, for at no other time was Valentinian likely to have permitted it. After the pacification had been concluded between Attila and the Roman legates, he fell back with his whole force towards Pannonia. At the passage of the Lycus or Lech, a fanatical woman, perhaps one of the prophetesses who are described as always accompanying the Hunnish armies, is said to have suddenly crossed his path, and, seizing hold of the bridle of his horse, to have three times cried out, "Back, Attila!", but notwithstanding that warning he continued his course to his Hungarian capital, from whence he was never again to take the field against the Romans.

66. Erroneous statement of Jornandes.

Having returned home, Attila sent an embassy to Marcian to demand tribute, whereupon Apollonius was despatched across the Danube from Constantinople to appease his anger. It does not appear whether he pacified him by gifts at that time, but money was probably paid.

Jornandes states that Attila proceeded afterwards by a different route from that which he had before followed to re-enter Gaul, and again attempt the reduction of the Alans on the Loire; but that Torismond king of the Visigoths was prepared to assist them, and defeated him once more on the same Catalaunian plain, forcing him to return home ingloriously. Notwithstanding the assertion of that writer, who lived in the century next after the events he related, the concurrent testimony of the Roman Chronicles, and the date of Attila's death make it certain that the story was as false, as it is improbable. It must have originated in the circumstance of king Torismond having succeeded to the throne during the victory of Chalons, which might therefore have been truly said to have been gained first by Theodoric, and after his fall by Torismond; and an interval of time being erroneously placed between the exploits of the father and the son, the same events were supposed to have occurred again at a later period. Gregory of Tours however relates that the Alans themselves were defeated by Torismond not long before his death, which took place in this same year, but he makes no mention of any Huns in Gaul at that period.

67. Death of Attila.

If the life of the Hunnish conqueror had been prolonged many years beyond this time, it appears as certain, as any event that human foresight can anticipate by the consideration of existing things and past experience, that the Roman empires of the West and East must erelong have been reduced to unconditional surrender of their authority, and that, without the intervention of some great and unexpected deliverance, Christianity, which had so lately become the law of the empire, must have been nearly stifled in Europe; but it pleased the Divine wisdom to cut short the life of Attila at the very moment, when the predictions concerning the termination of the Roman power, at the expiration of its 1200th year, seemed about to be accomplished by his elevation to the thrones of both Caesars, and the revelation of Antichrist was expected in his person; and with his life the mighty fabric which he had consolidated was immediately dissolved.

The innumerable offspring of his multifarious concubinage claimed participation in the inheritance of his power. They did not however succeed in wresting it from the children of Creca, who were his lawful successors, but the great warriors amongst his vassal kings were too valiant and preponderant to be long constrained by influence less authoritative, than that of Attila. The Gothic kings threw off the yoke; and Gepidian Arderic, who had been the faithful counselor and companion of Attila, and the bulwark of his authority, struck the fatal blow to that of the young princes, whom he defeated in a great battle near the river Netad, which is not identified, and took possession of all Dacia.

From that moment the ascendancy of the Huns was utterly extinguished. Ellac, the eldest of the princes fell in the battle, and Dengisich and Irnach fled to the shores of the Euxine. In the following year (455) Dengisich having the chief power amongst the Huns, in concert with Irnach, attacked the Goths as refractory vassals, but they were utterly defeated by Walamir, and a small remnant escaped to the strong defenses called Hunniwar in Pannonia. Irnach fled into Asia to a part of the Hunnish dominions called lesser Scythia, and his subsequent career was too insignificant to have been recorded.

Odoacer, who was destined to put an end to the Roman empire in the West a few years after, was a person of no great distinction in the Hunnish court at the time of the death of Attila; and Theodoric, soon afterwards king of Italy, was born from a concubine of one of the Gothic kings two years after his death nearly on the day of the victory gained over the Huns by Walamir. The account of a cotemporary writer preserved by Photius, states that he was the son of Walamir, who had prognosticated the future greatness of his son, by the emission of sparks from his body, a phenomenon by which the horse of Tiberius and the ass of Severus, (probably Libius Severus) are said by him to have presignated the elevation of their riders. Malchus and some other writers call him the son of Theodemir. Gibbon has followed the latter, and does not appear to have known the doubt which exists on the subject. A coin of Theodoric having the head of Zeno on the reverse, appears to testify, that, like Odoacer, he held the crown of Italy in nominal subordination at least to the Eastern emperor.

68. Nibelungenlied.

The particulars of the death of Attila are involved in considerable obscurity. The chronicler Marcellinus, who wrote in the next century, asserts that he was murdered by a concubine, suborned by the patrician Aetius, and indeed it is difficult to believe that any great act of political villainy should have been committed at that time without the privity of that unprincipled statesman. Jornandes cites from the lost history of Priscus, that Attila, according to the custom of his nation, (probably meaning only the privilege of its kings) having added to the innumerable multitude of his wives a very beautiful girl called Hildico, which is merely another form of the name Hilda, after indulging in great hilarity at the wedding, lay upon his back oppressed with wine and sleep; that a redundancy of blood, which gushed from his nose, having found a passage into his throat, put an end to his life by suffocation; and that inebriety thus terminated all his glories. This story was doubtless promulgated by his murderers, but is highly improbable, when we consider the great abstemiousness of Attila, recorded by Priscus; and, as marriage was to him a circumstance of very frequent occurrence, it is not likely that he should have departed from his usual habits of sobriety on this occasion.

Sigonius and Callimachiis state the name of the lady to haye been Hildico, but Olaus, Thurocz, and Bonfinius, call her Mycolth, daughter of the king of Bactria, and Ritius varies that name to Muzoth, while Diaconus, the Alexandrine Chronicle, and Johannes Malalas simply call her a Hunnish prostitute, by which opprobrious term the Christian writers would probably have styled any of his subsidiary wives. Johannes Malalas also says that the girl was suspected of having murdered him, but that others assert he was murdered by his sword-bearer at the instigation of Aetius. He is said to have struck his foot painfully, as he entered the bridal chamber, on which, addressing himself, as it was supposed, to the angel of death, he exclaimed, "If it be time, I come"; and on the night of his marriage his favorite horse died suddenly.

The most ancient legends of Germany and Scandinavia are filled with the adventures of Attila, and of the ever memorable Hilda (the Hildico of Jornandes) in a variety of forms, and with much confusion of circumstances and appellations. The celebrated old German lay of the Nibelungians treats of this matter. A great part of the poetical Edda of the Scandinavians is occupied with the detail of these transactions, and the old sagas called Volsunga, Wilkma, and Nifflunga Saga, are records of the same. A careful consideration of the old Scandinavian documents, together with the undeniable evidence of Priscus, that Attila ruled over the Northern islands, makes it pretty clear, that the Danes have no real history previous to the occupation of their territory by Attila, and that most of their ancient traditions are reminiscences of that mighty conqueror, (who was in some respects the Odin of the North, as he was also the Arthur of Great Britain) or at least blended with them.

69. Attila identified with Odin.

In the Heltenbuch we read of the emperor Otnit, certainly meaning Attila, and attributing to him a name almost identical with Odin. Odin or Woden having been worshipped by the Scythian tribes in Asia, and probably being one with the sword-God, of whose type Attila had possessed himself, the name would be naturally bestowed upon Attila by those who acknowledged his divine title. An ancient medallion represents Attila with teraphim or a head upon his breast, and Odin was said to have preserved the head of Mimer cut off which gave oracular responses.

Attila is named Sigurd in several Scandinavian legends; Sigge is a name for Odin, and Sigtun his place of abode, all being connected with the word Sigr, victory. Sigi the son of Odin acquired dominion in France according to the prose Edda, and Volsunga saga says he was king of the Huns. The Edda states also that Sigi's brother Balldr, who fell by an act of fratricide, (meaning Bleda) ruled in Westphalia. Those statements actually designate Attila, who was looked upon as the son or incarnation of the sword-god, being the only Hun who ever had power in France. It must be borne in mind that, while the oldest Northern legends connect Odin with the Huns, the existence of that nation was unknown in Europe till 78 years before the death of Attila.

The Edda of Snorro (Goranson's ed. p. 34.) states that Hlidskialf was the throne of Odin, and in Atla quida st. 14. the same name is given to the tower or dwelling-place of Attila. That Valhall was the residence of Odin is universally known; the abode of Attila bears that name in the Edda, Atla mal in Gr. st. 14. In the same Edda, in Sigurd. Fafh. 3. st 34, Hilda says that Attila compelled her to marry against her will; and in Brynh. quid, she says that Odin condemned her to involuntary wedlock. In Brynh. quid. 1. st. 14. and in Volospa it is said that Odin conversed with, and obtained responses from the head of Mimer cut off, but, in Wilkina saga c 147, Sigurd, who is unquestionably Attila, kills Mimer. That Odin and his followers were Asiatics, or Asians, as they are styled in the Edda, perfectly accords with the origin of the Huns who had so lately entered Europe; nor does there appear to be the slightest ground for the suggestion of the Danish historian Suhm, that Odin was a person driven out of Asia into the North of Europe by the conquests of Mithridates, except the antiquity which, without proof, he was desirous of giving to the events detailed in the Scandinavian records; whereas it is most probable that no such individual bearing the name of Odin ever existed in the North of Europe, though that opinion may not be palatable to the Danish antiquarians. Attila is called in the Edda the son of Buddla, a name which seems closely connected with Buddha, the Asiatic title of the God Woden or Odin. Buddla is stated in Fundinn Noregur to have conquered Saxony and established himself there, but not to have been himself a Saxon. The exclamation attributed to Attila, "Lo, I am the hammer of the world",' has evident reference to the Scandinavian hammer of the God Thor; and, as he is identified with the war-god, his sister and wife Hilda is the war-goddess, of the Northern nations.

According to Olaus Magnus, Hother (the same who according to the oldest mythology of the North killed Balder son of Odin, from jealousy, on account of a woman), was set on the throne of Sweden by his brother Attila; and Attila succeeded Hothinus, that is Odin. This Hother, according to Vegtam's quida (known as the Descent of Odin), in the verse Edda, was brother to Balder, as he is above stated to have been brother to Attila. Hother himself according to Vegtam's quida was killed by Ali, (sometimes called Vali) who in the old Swedish version is Atle, that is Attila, and in the Latin Atlas, another form of his name, son of Odin and Rinda; therefore all the three were brothers.

I entertain no doubt that this famous tale of fratricide refers to the known murder of Bleda by his brother Attila, with a duplication of the act of fratricide, like that which occurs in all the tales of the murder of Attila himself; the cause assigned for the first act of fratricide being jealousy, for the second, revenge. Olaus Magnus states in his appendix, that Attila hated the Danes so, that he set a dog to reign over them, (which has some reference to the account in the Provencal romance that Attila was himself begotten by a dog, and had canine features) and that he was betrayed by his wife, who robbed him, and fled from him, and conspired with his son against him. In p. 827, we find another Attila king of Sweden, who also conquers the Danes, and dies by murder. Olaus compiled his work from vernacular legends, and in these fables we cannot fail to recognize the reminiscences of the mighty Hun, and his close connection with Odin, and the earliest mythology and story of the north; and they are confirmatory of the fact asserted by Priscus, that he did rule over the maritime countries of the Baltic. But the Scandinavian mythology not only begins with Attila, either, doing the same things that are averred concerning Odin, or called his son, but it also ends with him; for the prose Edda concludes with stating that this Ali, Atle, or Attila (who is stated in c 15. to be the son of Odin, powerful in military valor, and in archery, which was the special weapon of the Huns), is to survive with Vidar the God of silence, after the destruction of all the other Gods, and reign as before upon Ida; that is, that Attila was expected to come again in power, as appears by so many accounts of him both under his own name and the romantic name of Arthur. He is the son of Odin, taken as the sword-god or spirit of war and victory; he is Odin himself, looking to his achievements upon earth. The strange tale of the deception of the Jews in Crete in the reign of Attila, by a person pretending to come in the power of Moses as he did, throws some light on the assertion that Ali or Attila was ultimately to reign on Ida, the Cretan mountain, which was a type of that in Asia.

70. Identified with Sigurd. Scandinavian Fundinn Norregur

In the Scandinavian legends the catastrophe of Attila's life is told and repeated under different names with some variation. In the first place he appears as the son of Sigmund, possessing a celebrated sword called Gram, and a wonderful grey horse Grana, under the name Sigurd, a Hunnish king, superior to all his contemporaries in martial prowess, the vanquisher of many kings in France, sojourning for some time with the Burgundian monarch, betrothed to and lying with Hilda, surnamed Bryn-hilda, the sister of king Attila, fraudulently giving her up to Gunnar or Gunther, prince of Burgundy, and espousing the daughter of Hilda surnamed Grim or Chrim-Hilda, and murdered at the instigation of the revengeful woman he had forsaken by one of the Burgundian (otherwise called Nibelungian) princes, but not before he had slain one of his assailants, and after his death she burns herself, together with much wealth and many of her slaves.

He next appears in the same legends as Attila (Atli), son of Buddla, a king victorious over the Saxons near the Rhine, espousing Hilda, surnamed Grim or Chrim-Hilda, the widow of Sigurd, and having not only the same wife, but the same sword Gram and horse Grana, and his wife excites another Burgundian prince to murder him, having previously served up to him at supper her own children by him, after which she attempts to destroy herself. Then she is conveyed to the court of another king who had married her daughter Hilda, called Svan-Hilda, where another catastrophe takes place, a child of the same name as before, Erpur, is killed, and she likewise orders a pile for the purpose of burning herself. The first half of the old German Nibelungenlied relates the adventures of the person called Sigurd by the Scandinavians, under the name Sigfried, his marriage with Chrim-Hilda, and his murder by the revenge of Bryn-Hilda.

The second part relates the marriage of the widow to Attila king of the Huns, her attempts to avenge the death of Sigfried on the Burgundian princes, and her destruction by Theodoric. It is strange that the Danish historian Suhm, although in his chronology he has made these events coincide exactly with the era of Attila, appears never to have suspected, or did not choose to perceive, that the Attila mentioned in the Sagas and Edda was the renowned king of the Huns; nor did it ever occur to him that Sigurd king of the Huns could be no other person. On the contrary, he supposes the Attila there mentioned to have been a petty king over some Huns settled in Groningen. That Attila, brother of Brynhilda and son of Buddla, was Attila king of the Huns is certified by the Nibelungenlied and the copious detail of his adventures in Wilkinga saga; and the Danish editors of the late edition of the tragic Edda are satisfied of that simple fact, though they see no further into the unravelling of their confused traditions concerning him.

That Sigurd the Hunnish king of the Edda and Sagas, the Sigfried of the old German poem, was Attila, appears indisputably from the following considerations:—He had the same wife, the same sword, and the same horse; he was king of the Huns, and the greatest warrior of his age; he was engaged with the Burgundians, partly in alliance and partly in warfare; he vanquished many princes on the French side of the Rhine: all which applies to Attila. He was exactly contemporary with Attila, according to the chronology of those who did not suspect their identity. He was not only married to, but murdered by Hilda, as well as Attila.

It is utterly impossible that such another king should have existed at the same period, and been engaged on the same theatre of action with similar success, and under like circumstances, without coming into collision with him, and that no vestige of such a character should appear in the authentic histories of the times, still less could there have been such another Hunnish king at the same time. His identity with Attila is proved by his renown and achievements, as well as by the catastrophe of his life; and in a still more striking manner by the assertion of Brynhilda in the Edda, that, if Sigurd had lived a little longer, he would have obtained universal dominion.

In Sinfiotla lok is found another form of the story of Attila. Sinfiotl is the son of Sigmund the Volsungian; he and Gunnar woo the same person, on which account he slays Gunnar, and in his turn is murdered by Borg-Hilda, said there to be sister to Gunnar.

In Oddrunar Gratr there is another version of the tale. Gunnar is surprised in an intrigue with Oddruna, sister of Attila, whereupon Attila puts him to death in a cellar filled with vipers, and has the heart of his brother Hagen cut out. In Oddruna, sister of Attila, intriguing with Gunnar, may be recognized, under another name, Brynhilda, sister of Attila, fraudulently married to him. In Atla mal and Ada quida, Attila is said to have decoyed the Burgundian princes to his court to avenge the death of their sister Brynhilda, who had burnt herself after they had killed Sigurd, to have cut out the heart of Hagen, and thrown Gunnar amongst the vipers, in consequence of which his wife, the sister of Gunnar, killed his children and himself, and tried to commit suicide. In the Nibelungenlied, instead of being decoyed by Attila, they go treacherously, at the instigation of Hilda, to murder Attila, and are put to death as above stated.

Volsunga saga treats fully of the history of Sigurd, and subsequently of Attila; and at the end thereof as well as in Regner Lodbrok's saga, the name of Kraka is given to Aslauga, the daughter of Sigurd, which tallies with that of Kreka, the principal wife of Attila, recorded by Prisons. In Wilkina or Niflunga saga, Attila appears under the name of Sigurd Swein, and the Burgundian father of Gunnar is called Alldrian instead of Giuka. After the death of Sigurd Swein his widow is married to Attila, who being disgusted with her atrocities, permits Theodoric to kill her with the sword in his presence, to prevent her, as he states, from murdering Attila; whereby Sigurd Swein is distinctly identified with Sigurd Sigmundson, and with Sigfried of the Nibelungenlied, whose widow is killed in the same manner by Theodoric. Afterwards a younger Burgundian prince, Alldrian, son of Hagen, entices Attila into a cavern in a lonely mountain, where he discovers to him the amassed wealth of the Nibelungians and of Sigurd, and succeeds in blocking him up in the cavern, and tells him to satiate himself with the riches he had desired. Alldrian then returns to Bryn-Hilda the widow of Gunnar, who had caused the death of Sigurd and receives him with high favor on account of his having slain Attila. This account tallies with that of the enclosure of king Arthur in Mount Etna, where he was supposed to be still living, and from whence he was expected to return and rule once more upon earth. In the same saga the affairs of king Arthur are mixed up with those of Attila, and in an earlier chapter Attila sends a messenger to woo Herka (perhaps the same name as the I Kreka of Priscus, wife of Attila, and called Cerca (by his Latin translators) under the feigned name of Sigurd.

In Saemund's Edda, Sigurd is called the Southron, agreeing with the appellation of halls of the south given in another passage thereof to the residence of Attila. The legend of Hedin is a confused inversion of the Attilane tragedy. The same enchantress Hilda is the occasion of bloodshed; Hedin, a name nearly identical with Odin, representing Attila, and Hagen, his antagonist, bearing the same name as one of the Burgundian conspirators. The tale is an inversion of the conflict between Attila and the Burgundian princes. That it belongs to Hunnish history, and not merely to the Scandinavian population, is clear, because Saxo Grammaticus says that Hedin fought a battle which lasted three days with the king of the Huns.

The ancient chronology of the Danes respecting the inhabitants of Scandinavia is in a great measure founded upon Fundinn Noregur or Norwegian origins, a genealogical work in the old Scandinavian tongue, evidently written in the reign of Harald Harfager, who first united all Norway under the dominion of an individual (in 888 according to Suhm), for the purpose of showing that through his female ancestors he was descended from all the great families of the North; from Odin, through one line, from Buddla, the father of Attila and Brynhilda through another, from Sigurd through another, from Norr, Gorr, &c. The Danish historians have shown much want of discernment in believing this fabrication. The falsehood of these genealogies, which were forgeries of great political importance to Harald, may be at once demonstrated by the descent from Sigurd, whose death, if he be considered as Attila, took place in 453, and, taken as he is by the Danish historians, is placed a very few years earlier, that is just long enough before to give time for the last events of his life to be acted over again under the name of Attila. Yet the pedigree gives, 1. Sigurd; 2. Aslauga, his daughter by Bryn-Hilda, married to Regner Lodbrok; 3. Sigurd the snake-eyed; 4. Aslauga, his daughter; 5. Sigurd the hart; 6. Ragn-Hilda, mother of Harald Harfager; allowing only five generations for the space of 435 years between the death of Sigurd, taken at the latest period, and the monarchy of Harald, which makes each person in the pedigree 87 years old at the time of the birth of the child that succeeds. Such an absurdity throws complete discredit upon the whole tissue of genealogies, evidently a clumsy fabrication to reconcile the North to the usurpations of Harald, and it strikes at the root of the whole frame of ancient Danish story.

In a note to a short poem at the end of Helga, I apologised for a supposed confusion in my Icelandic translations between Aslauga, the daughter of Sigurd Sigmundson, surnamed Fafnisbana, who lived in the fifth century, and Aslauga, wife of Regner Lodbrok, daughter of Sigurd Swein, asserted to have lived in the eighth. I now retract that apology, into which I was misled by the disingenuous chronology of Suhm. The Fundinn Noregur distinctly says that the wife of Regner was Aslauga, the child of Brynhilda daughter of Buddla, and of Sigurd Fafnisbana, who lived, by the assent of all writers, in the fifth century, and who was no other than Attila; and Nifflunga Saga, relating his death and the vengeance of Bryn-Hilda, calls the same person by the name of Sigurd Swein. The Danish historian, finding himself thwarted by the gross anachronism in the false pedigree of Harald, attempted to bolster it up by splitting the same individuals into separate persons in different centuries, ringing the changes on the names Sigurd and Aslauga; to such a degree could nationality and a desire to uphold the truth and authenticity of Scandinavian legends warp the understanding, and even apparently the candor, of an antiquarian, whose disquisitions were too minute to allow a probability of his not having suspected the imposture. The story of Regner Lodbrok is a blending of the adventures of the grand-father of king Harald Harfager (a northern sea-rover, killed in the eighth or ninth century by Ella in Northumberland), with some of the celebrated Attilane reminiscences concerning Hilda, Sigurd, and Aslauga, who may have been the younger Hilda; and consequently we read that the sons of Regner, with a great army, proceeded in his lifetime to Luneberg in Saxony, with the intention of marching against Rome, but abandoned the expedition on further consideration, a passage from the life of Attila, ridiculously misapplied to the offspring of a Northern pirate. The name Regner appears to have been Hunnish, for Agathias mentions that Regnar, general of the Goths, who attempted to assassinate Narses, was not a Goth, but of the tribe of Bittores, a Hunnish race. Regner Lodbrok himself is stated to be the son of another Sigurd (Sigurd Ring) and another Hilda (Alf-Hilda), so incessantly are the changes rung upon these feigned names of the sera of Attila. It appears that the poetical Edda had been written long enough before the reign of Harald Harfager for the particulars related in it to have obtained credence, and before the names Dane and Denmark were established in the north of Europe, probably at the close of the sixth century.

71. Result of a comparison of various traditions.

It will be observed that, in all the various versions of the catastrophe which cut short the life of this mighty potentate, a revengeful woman of the name of Hilda bears a conspicuous part; that some false play, by which she was dishonored, seems invariably to be the cause of her virulence, and that the Burgundian family are always mixed up in the transaction, with great confusion between an elder and a younger Hilda. Both Cassiodorus and Prosper Aquitanicus testify in their chronicles the fact that Gundicar or Gunnar, the Burgundian, was slain by the Huns not long after his treaty with Aetius, showing thereby that the later legends have some foundation in reality. The result of these various relations, taking into consideration that Priscus states Attila to have married his daughter Eskam, seems to be, that he, as told of him under the name of Sigurd, had a daughter by his sister Hilda, who is sometimes called Brynhilda, sometimes Hilda i bryniu, or the mailed Hilda, described as a warlike woman and enchantress; that he had betrothed himself to her, but not married her, and that he afterwards compelled her against her will to marry the prince of Burgundy; that he subsequently in 448 espoused the younger Hilda, (sometimes called Chrim or Grim Hilda, sometimes Gudruna or divine enchantress, as the other Hilda is also called Oddruna or enchantress of the arrow head) his daughter by his sister, (Brynhilda, sometimes also called Grimhilda) in consequence of which she, the elder Hilda, excited the Burgundian princes to attempt to slay him; but that he put them to death, and was afterwards murdered by a younger prince of that nation at her instigation; that the catastrophe did not take place on the night of his marriage with Hilda, but at a later period and on the occasion of another wedding, though the previous union with Hilda was the cause of his murder. Coupling these particulars with the account of Priscus, that in 448 he wedded his own daughter Eskam, of other historians that he died on the night of his wedding with Mycolth, and of others that Hilda was suspected of having murdered him, it seems not improbable that Eskam was the younger Hilda, his daughter by his sister whom he had compelled to marry the Burgundian, and through whose revenge his murder was effected, with the aid of one of the Burgundian princes, on the night of his marriage with Mycolth in 453; Gunnar, otherwise called Gunther or Gundicar, having been previously excited against him, and slain after an unsuccessful attempt upon his life. It is very probable, that Aetius was privy to the conspiracy, as Marcellinus has positively asserted.

The Wilkina saga contains the detail of a variety of exploits by Attila, his victory over Osantrix king of Denmark, with his gigantic champions Aspilian and his brothers, his conquest of Russia from Waldemar, and the defeat of Hermanric by his arms, some of which events may perhaps be founded in truth, but they are discredited by the anachronism of introducing as his coadjutor, Theodoric of Verona, meaning Theodoric afterwards king of Italy, who was not born till two years after the death of Attila; but, in this and in various other relations be has been confounded with an earlier Theodoric, or the actions of Theodemir the vassal of Attila have been attributed to Theodoric, who was either his son or his nephew. Hermanric the Ostrogoth had been probably dead before the birth of Attila, and the supposed victories over him, and the alleged cooperation of Theodoric, were perhaps connected with the fabulous account of Attila's great longevity; but the age of 120 years attributed to him by the Hungarian writers, being that of Moses, seems to have arisen out of the notion that he came in the spirit of Moses, and was in fact alter Moses.

72. Funeral of Attila.

According to the statement of Priscus, as related by Jornandes, the attendants of Attila abstained from entering the bridal chamber for a considerable time, thinking that he was pleased to lie late; but at length, after calling loudly in vain, having forced the door they found him dead, and the girl, whom he had espoused, dejected and weeping under the covering of her veil. Thereupon, according to the customary manner of mourning the dead amongst his countrymen, they cicatrized their faces, in order, as the historian says, that he might be bewailed by the blood of men, and not by the tears of women. A silken tent was pitched in the open plain, and there his body was borne and lay for some time in state; while the most distinguished of the Hunnish cavalry careered around him, in the manner customary at the games or tournaments of the Roman circus, in which the horsemen used to be divided into four parties clothed with uniforms of different colors, and they chanted during their evolutions his praise in funereal accents, saying, "Attila, the chief king of the Huns, son of Mundiuc, lord of the bravest nations, endowed with an extent of power unheard of before his time, having alone possessed all the kingdoms of Scythia and Germany, and terrified both empires of the Roman city, having captured or trampled on their towns and having consented to receive an annual tribute, being appeased by entreaties to spare those which were not yet sacked, when he had brought all those things to a prosperous conclusion, ended his life, not by hostile violence or by the treachery of his own people, but in the full enjoyment of the security of his nation, amidst festivities, and without any sense of pain. Who would not esteem such a termination of his life desirable!

After the equestrian exercises had been performed, and the dirge, of which the above substance has been preserved to us, had been chanted, they buried him secretly. He had three several coffins or rather biers, the first decorated with gold, the second with silver, the third with iron, signifying by those symbols that the three metals appertained to so powerful a king;

with evident reference to the prophetic monarchies of Daniel, the gold representing the Babylonian, the silver that of the Medes, to both of which he pretended in the title he had assumed, and the iron both the Roman empire, and the deified sword by virtue of which he ruled. He was interred at night, after which a vast heap of spoils was made over his tomb, or rather over his body; and they buried with him arms of his enemies which had been taken in battle, trappings studded with gems, and the banners of various nations.

After this ceremony, the Huns celebrated his funeral rites with profane feasting and wassail, and the supper is said to have been served up in four courses, the first on plate of gold, the second of silver, the third of brass, the fourth of iron, including the third or brazen Macedonian kingdom with the three others which had been before signified; and it is observable that the historians, who have recorded these remarkable facts, do not seem to have had any notion of their apparent mystical intention, and their ignorance of the secret meaning affords strong reason for believing their report.

The slaves by whose labor the grave of the Hunnish monarch was excavated, were put to death as a sacrifice to his manes, and, as Jornandes states, to deter curiosity from prying into and pilfering the wealth which was interred with him; but it is difficult to understand how the place of his interment could be rendered secret, even by murdering the workmen, if the tomb was covered with the spoils of nations, and it is most probable that the spoils were all buried and laid over the site of the body, and not over the tomb externally. With like view to secrecy and security, the body of Alaric had been deposited under the bed of the river Busentinus. The Hungarian writers say that Attila was buried near Kaiazo or Cheveshusa (a Hunnish word of Teutonic origin, meaning Cheve's house) where the Hunnish kings Cheve, Cadica, and Balamber, were entombed.

73. Attila identified with the king Arthur of romance.

The identity of Attila with the Arthur of romance has been pointed out by the author of Nimrod. It is by no means improbable, that, when the arms of Attila extended themselves successfully over the North of Europe, the Saxon sea-kings, whom he, being unprovided with a maritime force, could not reduce under his dominion, may have removed to England in some measure to avoid his ascendancy; and, although we have no reason to believe that Attila ever sent any military expedition into Great Britain, the Scandinavian legends say that his companion Theodoric sent Herbert his nephew thither to king Arthur, who can be demonstrated to be no other than Attila, to ask for the hand of his daughter Hilda in marriage, but there is a story of fraud wherever the nuptials of Hilda are mentioned, and Herbert in this account draws a frightful picture of Theodoric to disgust her, and marries her himself. It may be surmised, that, as it was natural for the Britons, who were sorely pressed by the Saxons, to apply to the great conqueror of Europe, he may have sent them assurances of his good-will and intention of succoring them hereafter, and have initiated them in his Antichristian pretensions and claim to universal monarchy.

From such secret communications the Druidical free-masonry may have originated; and Olaus Magnus, who styles Arthur king over Britain, Ireland, Scandinavia, Denmark, and the rest of Europe to the Palus Maeotis, which could not have been predicated of any man except Attila, mentions that he instituted certain families or societies of illustrious men, which seems actually to designate lodges of illuminati.

The following extract from a MS. by the author of Nimrod, which he has kindly communicated, will preclude the necessity of my entering further into this part of the subject. It seems to me clear that the Arthurian fable is a Druidical location of Attila, as bead of the Antichristian power, in Great Britain. "This topic may be handled to better satisfaction by showing to what real man and actions the unreal Arthur of Britain had reference, and why mortals so widely removed from the era of the lower Western empire, as those who seem to revive in his person, have been raised up, like phantoms, to cross our path in history.

The Arthur of romance was king in AD 452, and the siege perileux in the centre of the round table, bore an inscription that in that year the seat ought to be filled, and the quest of the Saint Grail achieved; yet Arthur failed of doing either. Bearing that date of romance in mind, we must observe that Arthur was armed with a sword brought to him from heaven, in right of which he was (like a second Orion) called Llaminawg, the sword-bearer. The celestial sword was so interwoven with his life, that, until it was flung into the water, he could not depart from this world for his appointed sojourn in Damalis or Avallon.

It seems to have contained the divine part of his nature. In Tyran le Blanc we read of Arthur imprisoned in a silken cage, having life, but void of knowledge and discernment, save that he could answer all questions by gazing fixedly upon the naked blade of his sword Excalibur. When that was taken from him, he no longer knew, perceived, or remembered anything.

That sword was his mind and his memory. Ireland, the Hebrides, Iceland, Scandinavia, Denmark, Germany and France, were conquered by Arthur, according to the accounts given in the Bruts and in Romance; he prevailed over the Roman empire of the West, and (as Leslie bishop of Ross says) over that of the East also. Attila king of the Huns claimed sovereignty over the Scythian and Sarmatic nations in right of the sword of Mars, not a weapon used by that God, but an idol of him, immemorially revered in Scythia, though seldom seen upon earth, of which he boasted himself to be the possessor. Most of the Northern nations seem to have been obedient to his power, and both sections of Constantine's empire were humbled by his arms into the payment of tribute. Arthur is stated to have passed into Gaul, and gained a great victory in Champagne over the roman general Lucius Tiberius, and was marching on to attack the Roman emperor himself in Italy, (whom Geoflrey ap Arthur calls Leo) when the intrigues of Medrawd the Pict, and Guenever recalled him home, and shortly after destroyed him. The Hun fought a great battle in Champagne against the general Flavius Aetius, and soon after marched against Italy, where he was encountered by pope Leo, and by agreement with him,(but for what private reasons I leave for historians to enquire) returned to his own country. This was in AD 452, the very same year in which the Romantic Arthur should have filled the siege perileux, but did not. A few months completed the life of Attila, by means (as it has been supposed) of an unfaithful wife and foreign or domestic treason.It may be asked, is it possible, that two celestial sword-bearers should have been thought, or even feigned, to spring up, conquer Europe, successfully assail the Roman empire, return home,and perish under circumstances so minutely similar, and a perfect correspondence of date? True it is that the Brutic Arthur bears date considerably later than the Romantic, but it also true that the later date is only a cryptographic expression or cypher to denote the earlier one. Arthur, say the Brute, withdrew to Avallon in AD 542, which three figures are merely an anagram of 452".— "Of Arthur the sword-bearer it is said that he disappeared mysteriously from the earth, to which he was one day to return; Niebelungenlied speaks of the disappearance of the Hun, as doubting whether he was swallowed up by the earth, concealed in the mountains, or carried off by the Devil; and a Norse saga describes him as being enclosed alive in a hollow mountain, amidst accumulated treasures".—"Alain Bouchard (Grand Chronique de Bretagne, fol. 53) pretends that one Daniel Dremruz or the Red-visaged, reigned in Little Britain from 689 to 730, carried his arms into Germany, was elected king of the Germans, and proceeded to Pavia, where he married the daughter of the emperor Leo,He returned to Armorica where he was the most powerful monarch of all the West. His title is equivalent to Florid-faced (Gwrid ap Gwrid Glau) an Arthurian title. He is said to have descended from the Earls of Cornwall, Arthur's native province. Like Arthur he had no real existence; like Attila he ended his career of conquest by an Italian expedition, but did not penetrate beyond the north of Italy, during the reign of an emperor Leo who did not exist at the time mentioned. The circumstances identify him with both Arthur and Attila".—"In a great lake near Nantes is an island called isle d'Un, meaning Hun, in which is a great stone with a hole in it, under which a giant is said to sleep, who contended against Christianity, represented in the person of St. Martin of Tours; and it is traditional that a virgin is hereafter to put her arm through the hole and raise the stone, and resuscitate the giant and convert him. Martin died before the reign of Attila, but was uncle to St. Patric, his contemporary. The sleeping Hun is evidently Attila, and the legend furnishes another proof of his anti-Christian character, and of his identity with Arthur, abiding in, and expected to return from, the island of Avallon".

74. Conclusions

It is much to be regretted that the particulars of the life of this conspicuous man have not been more perfectly preserved, but if we assume from what has been premised, that which I firmly believe, that the mythology and the early history of the North originates in Attila, that the Arthurian legends have like reference to him, and that the Antichristian expectations, which had centered in him, continued to be cherished in the mysticism of romances, giving a tinge to whatever literature did not spring from monastic sources, we cannot fail to perceive how great was the depth and durability of his spiritual influence and machinations, as well as his political power; and we may estimate what would have been the grievous consequences, if his career had not been cut short before he had had time to complete the subjugation of Europe and consolidate his Antichristian empire.

His character may be easily traced from his conduct and achievements. Simple and abstemious in his habits, he gave no cause to the humblest of his followers to look with an evil eye on his exaltation. He was hardy, strong, active, and distinguished in martial exercises; silent and thoughtful in his hours of festivity; his determinations were peremptory, their execution rapid and effectual.

Superstition and terror extended his influence, but the happiness of his subjects, his kindness, justice, and success, gave strength to his authority. He afforded safety to all who were overshadowed by his power, while he threatened certain destruction to all who resisted his dominion, and unrelenting persecution to all who fled from it.

The lamentable state of Europe, at the time of his accession, gives reason to conceive the delight, with which the industrious portion of the nations under his government must have hailed its protection; while the rapidity of his conquests, and the belief that he acted under a divine delegation, ensured to him the enthusiastic confidence of his soldiers. Partial and corrupt administration of the laws, tyrannical and ruinous exactions, inroads of barbarous marauders, wavering and imbecile policy, had annihilated the security of every individual within the limits of the Roman empire; and incessant strife, between the various nations who were pressing upon each other and upon the Romans for subsistence, had spread havoc and starvation without its confines over a large portion of Europe; but, wherever the ascendancy of Attila was established, the scene of bloodshed was immediately removed beyond its boundaries; the wealth, which he snatched by force of arms, or extorted by negotiation, from his opponents, continued to flow into his territory, and its interior presented an unexampled scene of contentment and security.

Attila was perhaps the mightiest of those, who have distinguished themselves for a few brief years on the theatre of earthly glory; and, if he had not been cut short in the plenitude of his strength by an overruling Providence, we have every reason to believe that he must erelong have obtained the undisputed possession of Europe, and neither the Persians of Asia, nor the Vandals of Africa, could have offered any serious opposition to the indefinite extension of his empire. But his personal influence was the magic girdle which held together the immense league that had been cemented under his authority, and the moment his commanding talents were removed by a sudden and unexpected death, the power, which had been a single-handed and resistless weapon in his grasp, appeared too mighty to be wielded by any person of inferior qualifications.

The establishment of his government over the habitable world was inconsistent with the spread of Christianity, and the Almighty will, which had sent him as a scourge on the population of the Roman empire, permitted him not to complete the overthrow of true religion; but annihilated by his decease the great fabric he had constructed, which was immediately dissolved by internal conflict in the absence of his absolute and decisive authority. The mighty one was gathered to his fathers; the power of the Huns, which had shed a baleful and meteorous gleam over the age in which he lived, was speedily obscured; their generation was lost, and their name extinguished; and the historian, after searching amongst the records of time for the imperfect relation of his achievements, is left to conjecture the city of his abode, the manner of his death, the place of his interment, and even the language that he spoke, and in which his decrees had been promulgated from the confines of China to the waters of the German ocean.

THE END

Printed in the USA
CPSIA information can be obtained
at www.ICGtesting.com
LVHW011249191023
761568LV00008B/218

9 781503 354524